RENDERBROOK

Renderbrook spring house (Spade Ranches Collection).

RENDERBROOK

A Century Under the Spade Brand

by Steve Kelton

Texas Christian University Press · Fort Worth

Copyright © 1989, Spade Ranch

SECOND PRINTING

Library of Congress Cataloging-in-Publication Data

Kelton, Steve.
Renderbrook : a century under the spade brand /
by Steve Kelton.
p.   cm.
ISBN 0-87565-083-X
1. Renderbrook Ranch (Tex.)—History. 2. Ranch life—
Texas—History. I. Title.
F394.R45K45   1989
976.4—dc20   89-5193
CIP

Designed by Whitehead & Whitehead

Contents

Introduction

The development of ranching in Texas from the 1880s forward was strongly related to two mechanical inventions which were born of Yankee ingenuity but found their true potential on the vast and often thirsty ranges of ex-Confederate Texas: the water-pumping windmill and barbed wire.

The hundred-year-old Spade Ranch has a unique tie to the history of barbed wire. It was established as an investment for earnings which barbed wire had brought to Illinois farmer-entrepreneur Isaac Ellwood. Though Ellwood did not invent the concept of barbed wire, his shrewdness and ingenuity in producing and marketing that concept made him by far the most successful of its early manufacturers and would have earned him a prominent place in ranching history even if he had not become a ranch owner himself.

After a full century, the Spade today still belongs to Ellwood descendants. Relatively few of the many investor-created ranches of that transition period between the Civil War and the turn of the century still remain in family hands, making the Spade Ranch unusual in that regard.

In other ways, the Spade has been a textbook demonstration of ranching's evolution over the past century from an often free-wheeling open-range, Longhorn-dominated industry to today's forward-looking specialized operations which survive by using state-of-the-art technology in genetics, nutrition, marketing and range science. The history of the Spade mirrors the ranching industry's slow but steady advancement from the horse-and-wagon era to the age of computers, crossbreeding and embryo transplants.

There is ample precedent for the Spade's staying up with or even moving ahead of the times. After all, Isaac Ellwood's barbed wire was in its day an example of revolutionary technology, destined to bring large ranches under a degree of managerial control never before possible. It allowed, even encouraged, upgrading of cattle through selection to produce a better quality beef animal. By rapidly closing off the open range, it prompted cattlemen to move toward land ownership because they no longer had cheap or free use of unclaimed state lands. It allowed farmers an economical means to protect their fields from other men's cattle and hastened the claim of the plowman to deep-soil lands which once had produced grass for millions of buffalo.

Isaac Ellwood and his son, W. L., longtime breeders of fine horses, applied their knowledge of genetic selection to the upgrading of Spade cattle by use of Shorthorn bulls and, some years later, upgrading the Shorthorns through use of Herefords. Recognizing the value of railroads to the region, W. L. donated a right-of-way at a time when some landowners demanded payment or even denied permission for the rails to cross their ranches. And when the automotive age came honking its way out of the East, Spade owners were not hesitant in adapting the car and the truck to the needs of the ranch operation. In a more recent time, the Spade was among the early converts to the concept of crossbreeding to combine the better traits of several breeds and produce a fast-maturing, easy-gaining animal that would yield leaner cuts of beef demanded by this generation's health-conscious public. And the Spade has dipped its toe into the ultra-modern concept of embryo transplants to hasten the multiplication of superior animals.

Early ranchmen lacked a solid benchmark for appraising the grazing limits of West Texas grassland, which to that time had been home mainly to the great migrating buffalo herds. Some grievously overstocked their ranges. W. L. Ellwood strove diligently to adjust livestock numbers to fit the grass and avoid abusing the land. Recurring drouths often defeated him and his successors on this score, but they tried always to learn from experience. Ironically, the barbed wire which made the Spade Ranch possible and, in many ways, was a boon to the industry was also a contributing factor to a long-term decline in range conditions because it confined animals to a given area and did not allow them to vacate an overused range in the way the buffalo always had.

The Spade has long been a follower of developments in range science, trying for itself such emerging management techniques as the Merrill rotation system and high intensity, low frequency grazing to improve the range resource. It has invested heavily in brush control and grass reseeding to restore the land as nearly as possible to the near-virgin condition Isaac and W. L. Ellwood found there a hundred years ago.

A ranch is always more than land and cattle. It is also people, and the Spade from its inception has been blessed by having employees who not only were well above average in their competence but, as a group, tended to stay for decades. The Ellwoods realized that their background as farmers and horse breeders was not enough to make them successful as ranchers in a West Texas that was far different from their native Illinois. They were fortunate in acquiring the services of Dick Arnett, an experienced Texas cattleman. Other Arnetts gravitated to the operation and remained, so that the Arnett family is entwined into the ranch's history as inextricably as the Ellwoods themselves.

There have been others of great longevity, such as the Northcutt family, and in particular Otto Jones, whose tenure on the ranch lasted sixty years. As a livestock news reporter I was privileged to know Otto Jones during the last three decades or so of his life; I had known his cowpuncher brother Fred when I was a boy. I was among several hundred invited to the ranch when Otto was honored for his first fifty years there, along with two other long-time Spade men, Will Eisenberg and Tom Arnett. That was at the time when the long 1950s drouth was breaking up, and no one complained—least of all the drouth-educated honorees— when a sudden hard shower threatened the barbecue.

The hundred-year history of the Renderbrook Spade Ranch is, in a major degree, the history of ranching in West Texas. That it continues into a second century under the same family's ownership is a tribute to that family and to the many loyal employees whose labor, intelligence and devotion have kept it afloat during drouths and depressions that brought ruin to many similar ranches. I am glad its story has been written, and that my son Steve was chosen to write it.

Elmer Kelton
San Angelo, Texas
May 1989

Cool Water and
Cold Steel

O N the third day of February 1872, Captain Joseph Rendlebrock led thirty-one men of Company G, Fourth Cavalry, out of the frontier post of Fort Concho, Texas.[1] It was to be a routine scout, like so many before and after; the troop would search for Indians and, barring that, Indian sign. In the process, they would explore the still little-known country west and north of Fort Concho, seeking out and mapping such features as Indian trails, gaps in the low-slung but rugged mountains, and water holes, easily the most important features in this arid land where even the rivers guarded their moisture with quicksand traps.

This particular scouting expedition would fade into history barely noted and virtually unremembered, but it would leave its leader's name—in somewhat garbled form—forever stamped on a freshwater spring and the ranch that grew up around it. Rendlebrock's troop marched roughly due north of the fort, skirted the scraggly little whiskey village that would one day grow into San Angelo, then turned slightly westward as they crossed the North Concho River. On February 8, having followed the North Concho for four days, Rendlebrock turned his column north, soon climbing out of the Concho Valley and crossing the divide into the Colorado watershed. He noted and mapped a gap at that point, and close by the first independent waterhole sighted by the expedition.

Once within sight of the Colorado, they began moving eastward, parallel with the river, in the early morning hours of the ninth. The land varied from gently rolling prairie to broken country with numerous draws and a few live creeks. Limestone rimrocks capped the surrounding hills and occasional lone prominences scattered across the valley. A fringe of mesquite brush and mostly hackberry or other scrub timber lined the watercourses, but the vast bulk of the surface was open short to mid-height grassland. Soils ranged from caliche on the higher ground to red clay nearer the Colorado, with some pockets of loam and large beds of straight sand.

Rendlebrock reported finding "several fine springs" along their route that morning, culminating with the discovery at noon of "a very large spring near the top and north side of a hill . . . four miles south of the Colorado." The site today lies a little less than two miles due west of State Highway 163 between Colorado City and Sterling City, about three miles southwest of the point where the highway crosses Beals Creek.

Investigation turned up "a number of Indian wigwams, campfires and within a mile around the spring numerous signs of horses. From this I judge that the spring has been for times a camping ground for the Indians," he continued, "when traveling, going to or coming from there marrauding expiditions [sic]."

Water from the spring flowed "first in a northerly direction then east through a valley," and the soldiers followed the creek to where "it formed several little lakes of considerable depth." Rendlebrock camped at one of those "little lakes" that night, and there was to experience the first and only real excitement of the two-week winter scout. It may also have helped put his name on the spring, and probably led to a persistent though erroneous belief that the spring was named for a soldier killed in an Indian battle there.

In truth there was a battle of sorts at the "little lake," but the only casualty on either side was "one of the four dogs belonging to the Company." The fight began shortly after midnight and lasted "less than no time." Rendlebrock estimated the Indians at no more than a dozen and reasoned that they attacked "for the sole purpose of stampeding my animals." They didn't press the issue, standing off about 200 yards, "sending up a loud and furious yell and firing there [sic] pieces rapidly into my camp." The troops were "quickly alarmed" by "the combined noise of there [sic] shooting and yelling," he reported, "and turned out with there [sic] carbines." The Indians "decamped for good" after "a few rounds had been fired into them."

Rendlebrock followed the Indians' trail due south toward the North Concho the following day, discovering another good waterhole on the way but never catching sight of his attackers. After several more days of fruitless scouting along the Concho and its tributaries, he arrived at Fort Concho February 17.

Had the brief skirmish with Indians occurred elsewhere or not at all, Rendlebrock's name might not have become attached to the "very large spring" which carries it today. As it is, the attachment suffered at the hands of poor spellers, being corrupted almost immediately to "Renderbrook." History doesn't record the culprit responsible for that transformation, but Rendlebrock himself may not have been entirely blameless. A veteran of two decades of Army service and, moreover, a native of Prussia[2] where military details are scrupulously observed, he nevertheless signed his report of this very expedition with the name "Rinde-brook."

Rendlebrock's judgment that the spring had "been for times a camping ground for Indians" may represent the sort of understatement typical of official military reports. Had he chosen to do so, he might have mentioned the walnut trees scattered along the hillside, already huge and ancient at the time of his visit.[3] Walnuts are not native to the area, so these presumably originated with nuts picked up by Indians far from the site and lost or discarded during a layover long decades before. From that winter day of discovery forward, Renderbrook was the white man's spring. Its earlier Indian visitors could literally count their continued access to its cool waters in terms of days and months, and then only during furtive stops, always pressed by the white soldiers who had come to haunt their heels.

Within half a dozen years the Indians' presence in the region would be so weakened that a white cowman would be living permanently—if somewhat primitively—in the shade of the Renderbrook walnuts. Inside a decade his successors would erect a substantial dwelling that survives intact today, take title to tens of thousands of surrounding acres and begin a barbed wire fencing project that would transform the open range cow outfit into a bona fide ranch with finite borders. Fewer than two score years after the cavalry's first visit, the man who made the barbed wire surrounding Renderbrook would own the land within, bought and paid for with proceeds from the sale of thousands of miles of such fencing. His heirs hold the ranch to this day, a century after his eyes first fell upon it.

In 1872, however, transplanted New Yorker Isaac Leonard Ellwood was still a world away from the rugged and dangerous West Texas frontier. Owner of a prospering mercantile and hardware emporium in the growing DeKalb community, he was well on his way to becoming a major force in the fertile farming country of northern Illinois. Had anyone suggested to him then that he would someday own one of the largest deeded ranches in Texas, Ellwood probably would have invited the poor confused soul in out of the sun.

I. L. Ellwood had already had his share of adventures, first working as a teamster on the Erie Canal and later following the lure of quick riches to the goldfields of California.[4] Settling down with a hardware business in a quiet Midwest farming town probably seemed a permanent end to adventure and excitement, but this tranquil phase was to prove only a springboard to far greater things.

Ellwood's store brought him into close contact with the farmers of the DeKalb area. It served not only as a source of supply for the machinery and tools they needed, but as a meeting place and social hub for such men when they ventured to town on buying trips. The storekeeper extended credit both on purchases and for personal loans, and he came to know his patrons' needs and their problems as well.

There was one need common to almost all of them, and the inability of Ellwood or anyone else to meet it was a nagging problem. From the time they first left the forested country to the east and ventured out onto the plains and prairies of the Midwest and beyond, farmers had found themselves increasingly short of adequate and affordable fencing. Where standing timber had to be cleared before farming could commence, abundant supplies of fencing materials literally grew on trees. Farmers had their fences before they had their fields. As the farm line expanded westward, however, it left the forests behind; timber that had been a burden to clear now came all too dear. Rail fences gave way to rough-cut lumber, and with increasing distance from the forests and mills, even this fencing became prohibitively expensive. Vast areas of fertile farmland actually proved more expensive to fence than to buy.[5]

The problem was compounded by increasing mechanization. As tinkerers and inventors developed new farm implements and the machinery to manufacture them at a reasonable price, ambitious men found themselves capable of breaking out, planting and harvesting ever larger blocks of land—if they could only protect it from their livestock and that of their neighbors.

With the machine age came at least one attempt at a solution to the fencing problem. Manufacturers had raised wire-drawing from an art to a science and eventually to a common commercial process. It became possible for farmers to string several strands of wire around their fields at a fraction of the cost of board fencing. Many of them did, but far more did not, especially after observing the results of pioneering efforts. Pitted against cattle, horses or hogs, slick wire fencing proved inadequate to the task. Hogs pushed under, horses over and cattle right through the middle.

Slick wire was a disappointment as a brute-force barrier, the approach that had always been taken to fencing. The notion that it might be used in some manner as a deterrent instead was a radical departure from conventional thinking in the mid-1800s. Lengthy patent fights that would be played out in coming decades produced abundant evidence that such notions sprang independently from fertile minds all along the frontier, but only one such attempt ever led to a lasting accomplishment. Judging from later developments it wasn't a particularly unique idea or even a very practical one, but it cropped up in the right place at the right time to catch the attention of the right people.

The place was the DeKalb County Fair, the time 1873, about a year and a half after Rendlebrock's discovery of the large spring near the Colorado. The people whom chance brought together then and there were the storekeeper Ellwood, local farmer Joseph Farwell Glidden, and lumberman Jacob Haish.[6] Taking in the sights at the fair, the three fell together before a fence exhibit belonging to a farmer named Henry M. Rose, of nearby Waterman Station. Rose had armed a piece of wooden fence rail with bits of sharp wire. The contraption wasn't a fence design as such, but was intended to be attached to existing fencing where necessary.

Rose had had a specific application in mind—his own "breachy" cow—when he devised his spiked rail, but he apparently wasn't blind to the potential commercial implications. He had shown the foresight to patent his "Wooden Strip with Metallic Points" earlier that year before presenting it at the fair.

History suggests that the DeKalb men took enough interest in Rose's invention to discuss it at some length that day. The fact that the armored strip approach was already patented apparently led them from the first to look for a different way to address the deterrent principle; at least the variations each of the men came up with would indicate that. And the similarities between their three independent designs implies that they jointly arrived at the idea of arming a wire fence during their discussion that day in DeKalb.

The three men worked separately on their fencing ideas for a while following the fair, but their paths were to cross often in the years to come. Two of the paths would merge, in fact, pleasantly and quite profitably. With the third, the frequent encounters through the years would be bitter and costly. Most historical accounts agree that Glidden took an early lead in the development of what was to become known worldwide as "barbed" wire, and it's entirely understandable that he did. A born tinkerer, he had the aptitude, as he was to demonstrate often over the years with patents on various devices and processes. And necessity may have prodded him on to invention. Part of the folklore surrounding barbed wire insists that it was actually Mrs. Glidden looking over his shoulder and urging an end to the depredations of pigs upon her garden.[7] Whatever the precise source of the motivation, it was effective.

Glidden made his first application for a barbed wire patent on October 27, 1873.[8] It was a thoroughly practical and simple design that would survive and eclipse almost all the improvements attempted later. In the few short months between the DeKalb fair and his patent application, Glidden had encountered and worked out the problems that had plagued would-be inventors before him—bugs that would later prove the undoing of many rivals who sought to tiptoe around his patents with different designs.

One of the first of his groundbreaking developments was a mechanical device to manufacture the barbs themselves. Evidently frustrated by the slow and tedious process of twisting his barbs by hand, Glidden converted an old coffee grinder to a new use. Mounting two metal pins in the end of the shaft opposite the crank—one centered and the other offset slightly—he fashioned a machine that would spit out uniform barbs as fast as he could feed the wire, turn the handle and snip off the finished product.[9] It wasn't a fully mechanized process beyond that point. A neighbor would delight in later years recounting how Glidden hired him as a boy to perch in a tall tree with a bucket of barbs and one end of a length of wire, fitting the barbs on the wire one at a time and letting them slide down to Glidden who would pinch them in place.[10] Glidden soon discovered a flaw in his design—the barbs wouldn't remain in place on the single slick wire despite his best efforts at pinching them. With nothing but friction to keep them anchored the barbs would soon loosen and slide from side to side. Perhaps even worse, the two-pointed barbs would also turn, rendering them ineffective. Glidden's answer again was brilliantly simple. He added a second wire, twisted around the barbed strand.[11] The barbs could neither slide nor turn beyond a few degrees either direction before the second strand stopped them.

This two-strand twisted wire armed with two-pointed wire barbs was the design Glidden submitted for patent in the fall of 1873. It was so good that it changed one potential competitor into a partner.

In the months following his patent application, Glidden had begun selling small lots of his new wire to neighbors. Word of the project soon reached Isaac Ellwood, who had been working on a design of his own. Curious about the other's progress, Ellwood made a trip to the Glidden farm early in 1874. Ellwood later said it took him only one long, sleepless night to conclude that the fence he saw along the road by the Glidden farm was superior to his own design.[12] Abandoning his design, Ellwood returned to Glidden with a partnership offer, and in July 1874, the two formally joined under the new banner of the Barb Fence Company.[13]

Half interest in the yet-ungranted Glidden patent cost Ellwood $265 and was to make him a millionaire many times over. It was a long uphill climb, however, and the seeds of determined opposition had already been planted—sown by the third man from the DeKalb fair encounter.

Lumberman Jacob Haish, like Ellwood, heard of Glidden's work, and like Ellwood, he investigated. Unlike Ellwood, however, he never admitted it. In fact, Haish apparently never even owned up to the incident at the fair. Professing himself "probably the chief factor" in the development of barbed wire, he declined to concede that anyone or anything had influenced or inspired his work. Glidden testified in later years that Haish "examined" his roadside fence within "a few days" after its erection in April of 1874 and returned the following month with "a mechanic" to take measurements of his wire-twisting machine. Haish's version, however, included neither of these visits. He maintained instead that he only heard of Glidden's design from "a friend," and that he immediately ceased work on a similar pattern and changed to another form, "concluding to let 'Uncle Joe' and what he was working at alone."[14]

But he didn't let "Uncle Joe" Glidden alone. Glidden's October 1873 patent application had beaten Haish by two months; the lumberman filed December 22, 1873, on a slightly different design. For reasons known only to long-dead patent clerks, however, Haish's patent was approved within twenty-eight days of filing, and Glidden's application still had not been granted as the spring of 1874 turned to summer. Meanwhile, Haish took steps to see that his rival's patent would never be granted. Armed with his own patent, he filed interference papers on June 25 against the pending Glidden application. This effort succeeded only in delaying Glidden's patent until late November, but it ignited a competitive war between the two developing barbed wire factions.

It may also have been the catalyst that melted the Glidden and Ellwood interests into one. If so, it was a serious blunder on Haish's part. An industrious workhorse and a born scrapper, Haish applied himself to the task of dominating the barbed wire business. He might have prevailed had Glidden been his only opposition; the aging farmer even then showed little sign of relishing the sort of battle that was shaping up. Ellwood, however, was an opponent to be reckoned with. Younger than either Glidden or Haish, Ellwood had already demonstrated a penchant for adventure combined with a shrewd head for commerce. And his ready recognition of the superiority of Glidden's fence design over his own marked him as a pragmatist who wouldn't let pride or ego blind him to reality.

Armed only with an "inferior" design, Ellwood would have been a hard man for Haish to run over. Possession of half of the superior Glidden patent made him a formidable opponent to challenge at all. In less than a year, the Barb Fence Company progressed from a rented building to its own two-story brick structure of substantial proportions. The new factory was steam powered and improved with a succession of patented production machines. Ellwood and Glidden added a salesman to carry their "Winner" brand of barbed wire to new territories, and took steps to ensure their company's future by buying interests in several "prior use" fencing patents that held potential for complicating their own patent.

For all its promise and innovation, however, the fledgling barbed wire business was still an "add-on" industry. The wire it used as raw material was bought in ever-increasing quantities from back East, where its manufacturers considered themselves to be selling a finished product. The swelling tide of orders from the DeKalb area was of more than passing interest to the eastern wire-makers. In February of 1876, Charles Francis Washburn, vice president of Washburn & Moen Manufacturing Company, Worcester, Massachusetts, journeyed west to investigate. He went first to see Jacob Haish, attracted in all likelihood by the lumberman's loud and lavish advertising. Impressed by the prospect of the new product, Washburn offered to buy an interest in Haish's company. Haish responded entirely in character, proposing a price of $200,000, a figure he later admitted was eight times what he would have accepted had Washburn only attempted to bargain. But Washburn wasn't there to play games. He flatly refused Haish's bold demand and took his proposal to the Barb Fence Company, where he found a more willing pair of prospective partners.

Ellwood was still vitally interested in the barbed wire business, but the aging Glidden found the prospect of retirement appealing. In May of 1876, Glidden sold his remaining half-interest to Washburn & Moen for $60,000 plus a royalty on future production. Ellwood had a new and powerful partner, and barbed wire took a fateful giant step from cottage industry to big business.[15]

The Opening of West Texas

Events were moving rapidly in Texas, too. Though somewhat tame in and of itself, Captain Rendlebrock's foray up the Colorado in early 1872 occurred during a period when Indian troubles were building to a climax. Less than a year earlier, May 19, 1871, the U.S. Army's official approach to the Texas Indian war had changed from one of denial and avoidance to active pursuit.

That was the day after a band of about 150 warriors, mostly Kiowas, attacked a train of freight wagons between Forts Griffin and Richardson on the edge of Young County. They killed six men outright and chained a seventh to a wagon tongue, whereupon they proceeded to roast him alive. One of a handful of surviving freighters, though badly wounded, reached the safety of Fort Richardson at Jacksboro, carrying the tale of the massacre.[1]

Federal officials up to that point had been inclined to dismiss Texans' stories of Kiowa and Comanche raids as no more than exaggerations of minor horse-stealing incidents.

Fort Concho (M. C. Ragsdale Collection, Fort Concho
National Historic Landmark).

The Civil War was still barely half a decade in the past, and despite frequent corroboration of atrocity reports by commanders on the scene, Army brass remained more interested in ruling Texas under the quasi-martial law of Reconstruction than in protecting its borders against Indians.

What lifted that particular attack, known as the Warren Wagon Train Raid (or Salt Creek Massacre), out of the growing pile of filed and forgotten reports was that General William Tecumseh Sherman happened to be at Richardson when the freighter was carried in. Sherman was one of those who devoutly believed the Texas Indian troubles to be exaggerated, but this time the evidence was staring him in the face. And perhaps more to the point, Sherman himself had been blithely touring the area at the time of the massacre. One contemporary account, in fact, maintains that the Indians watched Sherman's little party pass the site where they later struck the wagons. A medicine man had predicted that two groups of whites would pass and instructed the warriors to let the first go by because the next one would be more valuable.

If true, it was good advice in the short run; to the Indians, Sherman carried little of value compared to the wagon train and its teams. In the long run, however, it proved a tragic mistake on the raiders' part. Rudely robbed of old illusions by the narrowness of his own escape, Sherman vowed to change the government policy toward the Indians. Ordering Colonel Ranald S. Mackenzie into the field after the hostiles, Sherman traveled directly to Fort Sill on the Comanche-Kiowa reservation—along with his illusions about the severity of Indian depredations went any lingering doubt in Sherman's mind that the reservation had become a staging point for the raids and a refuge for the raiders. He fully expected their tracks to lead Mackenzie to Sill. And they did.

Confronted, the Kiowas confessed, and their bold and boastful admission of the heinous murders converted even the Quaker Indian agent to the general's new line of thinking. Government policy prohibited any action against these admitted murderers without the agent's consent as long as they were within the protective borders of the reservation, and such consent had never been given before. This time it was, marking the beginning of the end of the reservation as an inviolate sanctuary for marauders.

The next several months saw a succession of punitive and scouting expeditions, of which Rendlebrock's was one. Most were unsuccessful in terms of causing serious damage to the hostiles, but the soldiers' repeated presence reminded the Indians that their safe havens were shrinking. Perhaps even more important, each foray helped the shrinking process along by revealing more and more of the once-forbidding country's secrets.

Then, in March of 1872, the Army's knowledge of the Staked Plains took a tremendous leap forward. A troop out of Fort Concho captured a New Mexican riding with a party of Indians near the head of the Colorado. By his own account, the prisoner was a *Comanchero*, a trader in captives, stolen livestock and other Indian plunder. His information and cooperation revealed established wagon trails and waterings throughout a huge expanse of the Plains where the Army had never before ventured.[2]

Mackenzie spent the summer exploring, and in late September he discovered a large Comanche camp along the North Fork of the Red River high in the Panhandle. His attack netted him an estimated 3000 Indian horses and well over a hundred women and children. Escaping warriors recaptured the horse herd and some of the Army's mounts to boot, teaching Mackenzie a lesson he would later put to good, if grim, use. Otherwise, the campaign was a resounding success. It demonstrated to the Comanches that remoteness was no longer a guarantee of safety, and the women and children Mackenzie took prisoner ransomed back a large number of white captives as well as buying a winter of relative peace on the Texas frontier.

Typically over-optimistic, Washington officials apparently considered the Comanche problem solved. Mackenzie was transferred to the Rio Grande to deal with raids by remnants of the border tribes, and the last of his Comanche captives from the Panhandle expedition were returned to their families at Fort Sill. Their captivity had guaranteed the fragile peace, and the whites lost that leverage with their return. Raiding resumed at a frightful pace, intensified by a tenuous alliance between the Comanches, Kiowas and former Plains rivals including the Southern Cheyenne.

By late summer of 1874, only a few Comanches remained on the reservation; the rest had deserted to the Plains, and killings were recorded from the Texas frontier to Kansas. The Army was finally forced to act. Columns were ordered into the Panhandle from all directions, including Mackenzie's command from Fort Clark at Brackettville. He met reinforcements at Fort Concho and marched quickly to his staging area at Blanco Canyon on the upper reaches of the Brazos. On the way, he took advantage of the fresh water at Rendlebrock's spring. The converging columns fought numerous battles large and small before a series of fierce winter storms finally forced an end to the campaign in the last days of 1874.

The most decisive clash, however, was a nearly bloodless engagement early in the expedition. With the reluctant assistance of the captured *Comanchero*, Mackenzie's scouts had discovered a major Indian winter encampment under the sheltering walls of Palo Duro Canyon. At dawn on September 28, the troops began a single-file descent down a lone trail to the canyon floor. They caught the Comanches still in their robes, confident of the security of their hideaway. Only a handful of warriors could catch their mounts before the soldiers gathered the horse herd and started it thundering through the narrow canyon. The remainder, along with their women and children, took refuge where they could find it, struggling to escape up the steep canyon walls. Mackenzie's troops systematically destroyed the Indians' camps, burning tepees, equipment, robes and their entire store of winter food. They captured the horse herd nearly intact, and, learning from his experience of two years earlier, Mackenzie ordered the Comanche mounts shot.

The battle cost Mackenzie only one wounded trooper, and Indian casualties were light as well. Denied food, shelter, clothing and horses, however, the Comanches had no hope of surviving the upcoming winter on the Plains. Most retreated on foot to the reservation. The remainder of the winter campaign was mostly a cleanup operation.

There were occasional breakouts and sporadic raids over the next few years, but Mackenzie's deceptively easy victory at Palo Duro Canyon had broken the Comanche nation. West Texas was open to white settlement, and the whites wasted no time.

Some tentative grazing and stock-farming efforts had dotted eastern parts of the Concho country and filtered up the Colorado even before the Civil War.[3] For the most part, these were abandoned in the general retreat of the war years as the distant conflict siphoned off the manpower necessary to protect settlers against Indian attacks. The sprawling land still beckoned, however, and when the Indian threat was finally reduced, only the vagaries of nature could control the influx.

Foremost among those vagaries was rainfall. Farmers

had learned years earlier that the old delta-style cotton kingdom had no place beyond the fertile and swampy bottoms of east-central Texas. Those who moved into the limestone outcrops of the Hill Country and the Crosstimbers to the north had been forced to substitute a corn and stock-raising type of agriculture. As they pushed farther west toward the shadows of the Caprock, the progressively higher and drier land made even their staple corn crop a risky venture, and the focus shifted more and more to livestock. Some of the earliest inroads beyond Fort Concho were made by sheepmen drifting their flocks aimlessly and taking advantage of free grazing before others seized it.[4] It was the cowman, however, who claimed the lion's share of West Texas' limitless grass in those years, creating empires, legends and myths that would fire the imaginations of a nation for decades to come.

In those days before the windmill, rivers defined the range of most cow outfits, and natural waterholes were quickly snapped up as headquarters. That pattern was followed at Rendlebrock's spring. The first recorded operator to headquarter there was a man by the name of J. Taylor Barr.[5] His origin is obscure and his fate only slightly less so. Like most raw frontier regions, the upper Concho and Colorado valleys existed for the first few years of settlement without the legal framework that leaves official records.

One contemporary account indicates that Barr had a dugout at what was already known as Renderbrook Springs by at least 1878. Writing in the July 4, 1883, issue of the *Colorado Clipper*, H. R. Solomon mentioned various settlers he had encountered during a trip through the surrounding country in February of 1878. One of "less than a dozen inhabitants" of the area, he wrote, was "Taylor Barr, who died recently in Big Spring." Tax records for then budding Howard County carry a "J. T. Barr" for 1883. He is listed as owning $2200 worth of property in the town of Big Spring, along with twenty head of horses and or mules worth $815 and six pieces of rolling stock under the category of "carriages, buggies, wagons, etc." worth $750. No other land is rendered under Barr's name, nor any other livestock except a $6 hog, so presumably he was no longer running cattle as he must have been at Renderbrook Spring. The combination of town lots, vehicles and horses or mules suggests Barr may either have been in the freighting business or operated a wagonyard. A history of Howard County's first years supports the latter.[6] A list of early-day Big Spring businesses mentions a "livery stable" owned by J. T. Barr.

The same reference offers clues to support Solomon's vague report of Barr's death before mid-1883. In a discussion of a smallpox epidemic that swept the fledgling town late in 1882, the history cites commissioners' court records that show a payment of $2.50 to Barr for "a buggy obviously for hauling [a] victim's body to the cemetery."[7] That may have been the most costly job the liveryman ever undertook; the same page lists smallpox quarantines imposed upon the occupants of various residential establishments beginning on May 11, 1883, and Barr's house is one of them. Barr's name is absent from the Howard County tax roll for 1884, lending final, though highly circumstantial, support to the Solomon account.

Just when and why Barr left his dugout near the Colorado is unknown, but the identities of his successors are well documented. A 1930 treatment of Mitchell County history and its county seat, now called Colorado City but for years known simply as Colorado, puts the change of command at Renderbrook in 1875.[8] That is unlikely for a number of reasons, the least of which is that Barr himself wasn't even known to have been there that early. A far more plausible date is 1882, put forth by longtime Ellwood family friend, Judge R. C. Hopping.[9] Both accounts agree that Barr sold his open-range interests to brothers D. H. and J. W. Snyder of Georgetown. As for the date, Hopping's version came down through the years fairly directly from a former Snyder Brothers employee by way of the Snyders' own successors, the Ellwoods.

Hopping's chronology also squares with the few local accounts dating that far back, among them the Mitchell County brand records. These show that Barr registered a brand there on June 18, 1881, almost exactly five months after the county's organization. The first Mitchell County brand registration for the Snyders was early February 1882, followed six months later by D. N. Arnett, who served as foreman first for the Snyders and later for the Ellwoods.

Various accounts refer to the Snyders having bought the Renderbrook ranch from Barr, but along with the vagueness in dates is an even greater discrepancy in price. There is, in fact, no mention of price at all. Whatever the cost of the purchase, it must have been fairly nominal, because Barr didn't actually own an acre of the ranch in the first place. He simply grazed livestock on it, claiming range rights by the unwritten custom of time and place.

It was a custom already on its way out.

The Snyders left deeper tracks than their predecessors at Renderbrook. Dudley H. and John W. Snyder were Mississippi natives. D. H. was the elder of the two, born in 1833. Their father died in 1840, and a financial panic the following year left the family destitute. The father had left the family in what a contemporary described as "reasonably good circumstances" upon his death, but the fortune was mostly on paper in the form of interest-bearing securities that evaporated in the panic. Dudley Snyder in later years would tend to put his faith in more tangible assets, and he suffered his most serious reverses on the occasions when he did otherwise.

D. H. worked his way to Texas in 1854, trailing a herd of horses for a dealer who, he would later relate, taught him one of the most important lessons of his life. A man never makes money selling a horse, the trader said, "the money is made in buying it."[10] Snyder set to work collecting accounts for his grandfather, a pioneer merchant in Round Rock, and later turned his hand to farming and freighting. The latter enterprise evolved into a freelance business buying teams, wagons and loads of goods in Missouri that were unavailable in the raw young state of Texas, purchasing cheap Texas mustangs with proceeds from his sales, and trailing the mustangs back to Missouri to start the process all over again. Early in the Civil War, Snyder turned from trailing horses to trailing cattle, delivering several thousand head under contract to the Confederate Army. That exercise prepared him for a series of drives that would establish his fortune.

Snyder assembled his first post-war herd from Burnet, Llano and Mason counties in the spring of 1868 and pointed them northwest, past the head of the Concho, across the Pecos and on to New Mexico and Colorado. He pushed a herd to Abilene, Kansas, the following year, and in 1871 began a series of drives to Wyoming. His 1873 drive arrived at Cheyenne to find the country in the midst of yet another panic which had developed full-blown during his weeks on the trail. Snyder's intended buyers were bankrupt and the same prospect faced him; his assets were tied up in a herd of cattle no one could afford to buy.

Memories of his family's plight three decades earlier surely weighed on his mind, but Snyder gambled on a critical difference between the two situations: his mother had held worthless paper and he was holding worthless cattle. The paper would never regain its value but his livestock would, if he could only keep them alive long enough. In the worst of financial panics there is still money to be had for those who can afford the terms. Dudley Snyder found enough—at a staggering interest rate of thirty-six percent— to carry his cattle through the bitter Wyoming winter. They made him a nice profit the next year once the clouds of economic doubt had cleared.

Younger sibling J. W. joined Dudley Snyder at some point during these enterprises, and by 1877 the operations were known as "Snyder Brothers." They went into partnership that year with Denver banker J. W. Iliff for delivery in Colorado of 17,500 head of two- and three-year-old Texas steers, a deal which swelled to 28,000 head by the end of the trailing season. Iliff's untimely death thrust the Snyders into management of their partner's vast estate and perhaps whetted their appetites for empire. If so, it may have planted the seed that grew into Renderbrook. Whether it was their experiences managing the Iliff estate or simply a clearheaded realization that the newly opened range in West Texas would soon remain open only to those who held papers on it, something prompted the Snyders to begin buying land when others about them were content to graze it for free.

By 1882 the brothers and other Snyder family members were firming up title to thousands of acres in the vicinity of Renderbrook Spring.[11] Much of the land lay in Mitchell County, but parts extended into Coke and Sterling counties as well. There were gaps, but the Snyders held solid control over a broad expanse of range watered by the Colorado River and numerous creeks as well as Renderbrook and several lesser springs. Deeds in hand, the Snyders began improving their West Texas holdings. Accounts generally agree that there was considerable room for improvement. Taylor Barr's headquarters was described in Solomon's reference simply as a "dugout," the sort of structure common to such temporary holdings. Hopping offers more detail, citing a "building of two rooms constructed of chittum poles, a dirt floor, and a thatched roof."[12] The Snyder brothers added a substantial headquarters building known in later years as the "White House," and by 1883 erected a bunkhouse. They also began fencing, which allowed them to upgrade native Longhorn cattle with Shorthorn, or Durham, blood.

During this time they continued their drives to the Northwest, and they continued their partnership with Iliff's widow. The Snyders' final drive was in 1885, and its end coincided with the beginning of a third financial panic. This one cost them dearly, reportedly because they turned down a favorable offer for the Wyoming partnership at the request of Iliff Estate members. The value of their allied holdings plummeted soon after they allowed that offer to pass them by.

On the heels of the panic came a drouth beginning in 1886 and lasting into 1888. The Snyders didn't attempt to outlast it; in July of 1887 their Renderbrook cattle were among the first to reach the virgin range of the XIT Ranch, a sprawling tract of Panhandle conveyed by the state to a syndicate of investors who had provided cash to build the new pink granite state capitol building. Hard on the heels of land ownership and fencing, the investor-owned XIT was a harbinger of the next wave in ranching.

Capital requirements for land, livestock and improvements (wells, windmills and tanks, for example) quickly outran the reach of most of the men who had built the beef cattle industry. They were forced to turn to absentee investors for help in picking up the slack, either as partners or outright purchasers. Outfits like the Matadors, which sold to a Scottish syndicate, and the Pitchfork, financed out of St. Louis, were examples of the trend. Even pioneer cow-man Charles Goodnight was compelled to take on Irishman John Adair to help him hold his JA Ranch.

Pressed by the 1885 panic and the drouth that followed, the Snyders were looking for a buyer for Renderbrook when Isaac Ellwood and his son, William L., arrived in the little West Texas town of Colorado in 1889.

Birth of an Empire

WHETHER the Ellwoods were aware of Renderbrook's availability before their arrival is unknown, but they need not have been to have made the trip.

Judge Hopping's recollections maintain that their Texas excursion was to a great extent intended as a market development tour of the burgeoning ranch country. West Texas was at that time a major and growing outlet for their wire, and the Ellwoods, Hopping recalled, "decided to make a trip to Texas to get acquainted with the ranchmen. They felt this would be a help to their . . . business and at the same time they would look out for a location for themselves."[1]

I. L. Ellwood's share of the booming barbed wire industry had made him a wealthy man in only a few short years, and by the late eighties he was ready to invest some of the surplus beyond Illinois. Already renowned as a horse breeder and as the operator of a progressive farm complex on the outskirts of DeKalb, Ellwood's search for a new project naturally leaned toward the agricultural. Whatever the exact priorities, the father and son team detrained first

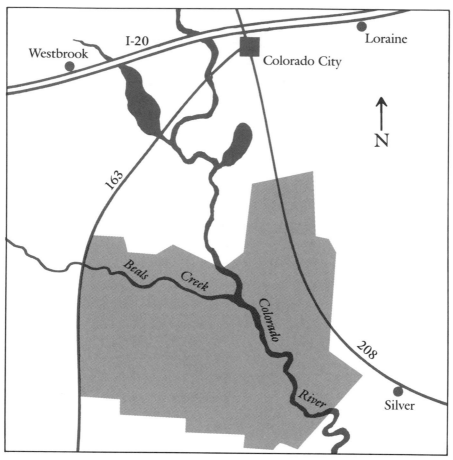

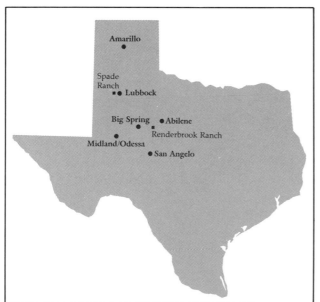

RENDERBROOK

See page 58 for map of Spade Ranch.

at Fort Worth, adding their longtime salesman Henry Sanborn to the retinue.[2] Within a few days the trio boarded the
Texas and Pacific bound for Colorado. The rails had reached
that point only eight short years before, but even then it
was a major gathering place for stockmen, having served
first as a supply point for buffalo hunters preying upon the
last of the southern herds. Between the arrival of the railroad and the arrival of the Ellwoods, Colorado had also
supplied the growing ranches northward, including the
southern end of the XIT. With or without Renderbrook as a
specific drawing card, Colorado was a logical destination
for the barbed wire moguls.

They headquartered at the St. James Hotel, another logical choice because of its similar use by area cattlemen. Most
cowtowns naturally developed a sort of "hostelry heirar-
chy," with big operators frequenting the poshest, smaller
ranchers congregating at a more modest establishment, and
cowhands gathered at a facility more suited to their meager
bankrolls. In fact, the need to do business dictated the
choice of all the classes. Cowboys and foremen were hired
in bars and hotels, cow trades were made, and barbed wire
was sold. And no small number of ranches changed hands
in the lobbies of classier cowtown hotels from Fort Worth
west. In Colorado, the St. James was where the big men
met.

Sanborn "talked up" their product, in Hopping's words,
and his bosses met many of their clients. Whether the Snyders were among their new acquaintances is unclear. Hopping says yes, and that it was on this first visit that the
Ellwoods inspected Renderbrook. Hopping's own account,
however, includes clues suggesting that the Snyders neither accompanied them on that inspection nor were on
hand to receive them at the ranch.[3] He describes the Ellwoods' traveling conveyance as a hired "canvas-topped

hack" supplied with "a couple of bedrolls," which suggests they traveled alone. Once at Renderbrook, he adds, they learned the history of the outfit from "a Mr. Root, who worked for the Snyder brothers." Had the Snyders been on hand in Colorado to meet Isaac and W. L. Ellwood, it seems only logical that at least one of the prospective sellers would have personally conducted their potential buyers on the Renderbrook tour.

In attributing the origin of the ranch's history to Root, Hopping implies that even Foreman Frank Yearwood may have been elsewhere at the time of the Ellwood visit. This lends credence to the possibility that the Ellwoods undertook the inspection on their own, perhaps learning of Renderbrook's availability from town talk. That is not improbable for an age when the grapevine served in place of today's instant communications and rapid transportation. As for the apparently hospitable reception the Ellwoods received at the ranch, it also fits the temper of the time and place; travelers, bidden or otherwise, were rare and genuinely welcome under cow-country custom. Even suspected outlaws often enjoyed a measure of hospitality, and a potential buyer during the tough times of the late 1880s might well have been courted like royalty.

Whatever particulars may have led them to Renderbrook, Isaac and W. L. Ellwood liked what they saw. The headquarters boasted the Snyders' house, only about seven years old at the time, and a lumber bunkhouse a year newer. There were also, of course, the spring, and remnants of Barr's old dugout along with decaying remains of buffalo and cattle hides that the early owner had stacked as a windbreak. The Ellwoods saw as well some tanks, the fencing constructed by the Snyders to that point, and doubtless some corrals, though no reference to these or to any sheds or outbuildings has survived.

Mostly what they saw, however, was potential.

Hopping wrote that they "believed that this was the place for them to carry out certain plans that had been revolving in their minds. This ranch was in its natural state, and they could improve it according to their own ideas."[4] Hopping's description of the actual purchase negotiation again indicates the Snyders were conveniently located at Colorado during the Ellwood visit, an account at odds with their apparent unavailability at the ranch. After returning to town, he wrote, the Ellwoods "soon worked out a business proposal to make to the Snyder brothers." They decided "to sleep on their plans," he continues, and "upon rising they called the Snyders to their room, presented their proposition, reached a quick agreement, and called in a local lawyer to draw up the contract."[5]

This story has a somewhat more anecdotal than historical ring to it for a number of reasons. There is first the nagging inconsistency regarding the Snyders' whereabouts; why, if they were so handy and anxious that they could be "called" to the Ellwoods' room the morning after the buyers' return to Colorado, were they not handy and anxious enough to have accompanied those buyers to the ranch? The story also implies that I. L. and W. L. Ellwood waited until the evening of their return to work out their purchase proposal. It seems more likely that such a proposal would have been pretty well fleshed out during the horse-drawn tour of the ranch and the twenty-five-mile drive back to town. The return trip alone should have consumed the better part of a long day through scenery already fully digested on the way out. With nothing to occupy their attention, the Ellwoods would have had hours to devote to discussing their purchase plans. Finally, there's the matter of the purchase terms themselves. Aside from noting that "the Snyders retained their cattle and

I. L. Ellwood (Spade
Ranches Collection).

W. L. Ellwood (Spade
Ranches Collection).

brand," Hopping provided none of the particulars. Most notably, he failed to mention a price.

A Mitchell County history says the Ellwoods paid "$1 million and a stud horse" for their purchase of the Snyder land,[6] but the magnitude of the cash figure makes such a deal unlikely. I. L. Ellwood was a noted horse breeder by that time, and the Snyders were known to favor good horseflesh, so the animal might well have been a sweetener in the deal. At a million dollars, however, the remainder of the deal would have needed no sweetening in 1889. That figure would have amounted to nearly $7.70 per acre for Renderbrook's original 130,000 acres.

No successful Yankee businessman would have fallen for a deal like that when the three-million-acre XIT had ended up costing its investors roughly $1.07 per acre hardly a year earlier.[7] And that cost was perhaps twice the going price for the times, a consequence primarily of cost overruns and unanticipated expenses arising from the capitol construction project. The highest outright bid for the choicest part of the capitol reservation, sold to pay for surveying the rest, was just over 55 cents per acre.[8] Only six years before the Renderbrook trade, Goodnight and Adair had purchased their sheltered, watered and virgin JA in the Palo Duro for twenty cents per acre.[9]

After a side trip to the Panhandle to look over the Frying Pan Ranch owned by Sanborn and Ellwood's old partner, Glidden, the duo returned by train to DeKalb. It had been a month-long trip, the first of many such excursions.

The next one began soon after for W. L. With the demands of the wire business and fall harvest details occupying his time, Isaac Ellwood turned to his older son to deal with the Renderbrook operation. There was a long string of improvements to get underway and, most pressing, the ranch needed cattle to replace those the Snyders retained under terms of sale. Accompanied by his wife, W. L. set out for Colorado, Texas, in the fall of 1889.[10] Once again he headquartered at the St. James, but this time his work took him far from town for lengthy stretches of time. One of his first acts was to hire W. L. Carpenter as foreman to replace Yearwood, who remained with the Snyders. Carpenter in turn rounded up fencing crews and a group of tankers with teams and two-horse scrapers, who set to work enlarging Renderbrook's already respectable list of waterings.

Next came the stock. From some source W. L. discovered that J. F. "Spade" Evans was offering a herd of Durham-cross cows off his ranch in Donley County near Clarendon. A contemporary of Goodnight and the other early cowmen, Evans was well known and respected throughout West Texas as an organizer and first president of the Panhandle Stock Association, which came to life early in 1881 to combat rustling. Leaving his wife to entertain herself at the St. James, W. L. Ellwood gathered a buckboard and driver at Renderbrook, threw in a camp outfit and headed north. At the end of the 200-mile trip he found the cattle he was looking for, and bought 800 head on the spot.

The Evans cows carried the "Spade" brand on their left sides, giving rise to their original owner's nickname. That brand would also stamp a second name forever on Renderbrook. W. L. hired Jack Hall of Amarillo to drive his new herd south and returned to register the family's new brand in Mitchell, Coke and Sterling counties.

The two-week cow buying trip confirmed Mrs. Ellwood's growing feeling of loneliness, and she soon decamped for their home and family in DeKalb, leaving W. L. to finish his Texas business for the year. The Spade cows were only a start in stocking the ranch, and a great number more would be needed. The Ellwoods would also need bulls, and their stock raising experience in Illinois dictated that only good blooded bulls would do. That, however, was one of Isaac's favorite projects, so the son put off such purchases until later. He contented himself with getting the Spade cows settled at various waterings once they arrived, then turned the winter chores over to Carpenter and boarded the train for home.

Stocking resumed the following spring, along with various ongoing improvement projects. W. L. devoted much of the next two years to scaling down his Illinois horse operation to leave more time for the ranch. That was a fortuitous decision, because 1891 saw expansion and changes that would demand much of his attention.[11] That spring, Isaac and W. L. returned together to Renderbrook to find themselves in need of a new foreman; for reasons of his own, Carpenter wanted out. That left the Ellwoods in a serious dilemma. They were now cattlemen on a large scale, but their knowledge of large-scale cow operations was still in its infancy. Even if one or the other lived on the ranch full-time, they would need expert counseling to avoid possibly disastrous pitfalls. As it was, neither of the Ellwoods could be on hand personally year-round. They needed not only a cow-wise counselor, but an on-site representative they could trust implicitly. With only tentative knowledge of the cow camp fraternity, they also needed advice just to find help. Apparently they turned for assistance to the Snyders, themselves veterans of far-flung enterprise. The result was perhaps more than they had bargained for. Not only did the Snyders put Isaac and W. L. Ellwood onto a foreman whose skills would serve them admirably for years, they also proposed another land purchase that would nearly double the Ellwoods' Texas ranch holdings.

The foreman the Snyders suggested was David Nathan "Uncle Dick" Arnett. Born January 20, 1847, near Cameron

D. N. "Uncle Dick" Arnett and his wife, from a picture probably taken in the 1890s (Southwest Collection, Texas Tech University).

in Milam County, Arnett was a member of a family of confirmed "westerers."[12] His forebears were thought to have
landed first in Maryland, moved to South Carolina and
then Alabama before migrating to Texas about the time of
the Texas Revolution. D. N. himself was barely a teenager
during the Civil War when he enlisted in a "home guard"
rifle company patrolling the frontier against Indians. He
had initially attempted to enlist in the Confederate Army
but was rejected because of his age. In 1864, when he
turned sixteen, Arnett traded his Indian-fighting role for a
job in the "real war," and served for the duration.

Still eager for excitement when the war was over, he
joined the Texas Rangers under Captain W. J. Motley in
1867. He fought Indians and outlaws for two years. Officially, he resigned his commission then to help his father
with a herd of cattle, but 1869 was also the year that the
harsh but basically fair post-war military occupation of
Texas gave way to rule by political radicals, the hated car-
petbaggers and scalawags. The state police force was one of
the first official bodies to be corrupted, and all but a bare
handful of the decent officers and troops either resigned as
Arnett did or were turned out to make way for political
cronies, bullies and outright criminals.[13] Arnett drove a
herd of cattle to San Diego, California, in 1870 and another
to Kansas in 1871. By 1877 he was piloting herds to Wyoming for the Snyder brothers, and in 1881 they made him
manager of their Yellow Wolf Ranch in Coke County, not
far from Renderbrook.

The country was still wide open at that time, and Arnett
soon built a herd of his own, registering the Scissors A
brand in Mitchell County in 1882. He ran both operations
from the Yellow Wolf headquarters until 1884, when he
moved to the young community of Seven Wells in Mitchell
County for school advantages for his children. Arnett was

apparently still in charge of the Yellow Wolf Ranch, running it long distance, when the Snyders recommended him to the Ellwoods in 1891. Leaving his oldest son, Sam, to take care of the Scissors outfit, Uncle Dick Arnett packed the rest of his family up and moved to Renderbrook.

In the course of their consultations over Arnett, the Ellwoods also discovered that the Snyders were offering another ranch for sale. Roughly 128,000 acres, it lay mostly in the Panhandle counties of Lamb and Hockley with some spillover into Lubbock and Hale counties.[14] Panhandle land was becoming a strong prospect for investment purposes as western parts of the state rapidly settled; its deep soils and abundant subterranean water supplies led to confident forecasts that farming would prosper. The Capitol Syndicate (the XIT owners) had just such a future in mind for its three million acres, and Isaac Ellwood's decades of experience in the Illinois farm country doubtless gave him a good feel for the dollar difference between range and farm acreage.

One of Arnett's first assignments under the Ellwoods was to accompany them to the Panhandle and assess the situation there. Conversion of the Snyder tract to farms would have to await better transportation and heavier settlement, which would take time. The Ellwoods wanted their cow-savvy new foreman to apprise them of its value as ranchland for the interim.

The trio made the trip by buckboard, carrying bedrolls and camp equipment. Hopping describes the journey to Lubbock as a two-day affair with a midway camp on a still-cool 1891 spring night. They made Lubbock's Nicolet Hotel the second night, then set off the following morning for the ranch camp about forty miles northwest of town. There they met with the Snyders' foreman, Frank Norfleet, whom Hopping described as "a man with a mind as bright as a silver dollar and an eye like an eagle. He could point out the camps where our own beef was eaten as well as the camps where the other fellow's beef was eaten."

Norfleet's job was to guide Arnett and the Ellwoods over the Snyders' Panhandle ranch, showing them both the expanse of level, treeless land and its sparse improvements. In contrast to his vagueness about the terms of the Renderbrook deal, Hopping recorded that the Snyder brothers were asking $2.50 per acre for the northern outfit. That would still have been a princely sum for the times, but not unreasonable, perhaps, given the growing speculation over farm colonization.[15]

The Ellwoods declined to rush into the deal despite their interest. Instead, they returned to DeKalb, and the result of their deliberations there may have provided the nucleus for the idea that the Renderbrook purchase included a horse trade. What they found upon their return to Illinois was that the horse business had slowed down. For years the Ellwoods had been importing blooded European horses to stock their breeding program, but they weren't the only ones doing so. Apparently, the market was reaching the saturation point. Trimming back the horse operation would give them both the time and the liquid capital to expand their ranching interests, and they came up with a plan that would shortcut even a portion of that process. By mail, the Ellwoods offered the Snyder brothers part of their asking price in imported horseflesh.

The proposal was accepted, and the Ellwoods returned to Texas in June to close the deal. The Snyders received their horses at Brownwood, and Hopping records that another carload went on to Colorado City for use in the newly expanded Ellwood ranching operations.[16] Once again the Snyders retained ownership of their cattle in the trade, reportedly selling these, too, to the XIT. Among the assets that went over to the Ellwoods was Norfleet, however, whose familiarity with the land would prove highly useful when it came to the daily mechanics of restocking.

With Arnett in charge at Renderbrook, Norfleet at the Spade—as the Panhandle ranch was designated—and W. L. Ellwood in general command, "Colonel" Isaac Ellwood returned to DeKalb. Isaac Ellwood's final advice when he turned the ranches over to his son and left for home was to "get the best" in cattle and materials. "There is no better grass country anywhere," he said in regard to stocking, and any improvements erected should be built to last. They were. Most of the essential headquarters buildings at Renderbrook were completed by 1892, including barns, sheds, corrals and chicken houses. A new kitchen and dining room were added to the Snyders' main house which, with a fresh coat of paint, became the "White House."

On the Spade, waterings were the first priority, along with fencing. Arnett shifted temporarily from Renderbrook to the northern outfit to supervise the windmilling, tanking and fencing crews, and the elder Ellwood shipped the necessary fencing materials south from Dekalb. There were still no rails into the Panhandle country, so all such materials were freighted by wagon from Colorado City. As this work progressed, W. L. devoted most of his time to locating and buying the good grade of cattle his father had insisted upon. During the summer and fall of 1892, crews of cowboys fanned out across the country trailing the new stock in, receiving and branding. It was a taste of the sort of activity that would soon consume W. L. Ellwood's time and attention almost full-time—an enterprise he would enjoy for the rest of his life. Cow work drew to a close finally as winter approached, and W. L. again mounted the steps of a T&P passenger car bound for DeKalb. He had been away from his family a long time, but ranching was seeping into his blood.

Colonel Ike

W. L. ELLWOOD would increasingly shape and mold the family's ranching interests, but his father was the man in whose pattern he would shape them. It was a unique pattern. "Colonel Ike," as he was often known after appointment to the Illinois governor's staff of advisors,[1] combined a strong sense of public and private morals with shrewd business acumen. He parlayed the chance event at the DeKalb fair—through a $265 investment in Glidden's patent—into substantial interest in what would eventually become the United States Steel Corporation,[2] one of the largest single business entities in the world at one time. In so doing, he was forced to overcome some determined and ruthless competition—both legitimate and illegitimate—eventually joining forces with some of his strongest opponents to overcome the remainder. The battle lasted for years, in great part because of Ellwood's own integrity.

As early as 1874, Ellwood and Glidden had taken on Henry Sanborn, a Glidden relation, as salesman for their "Winner" wire. Sanborn had worked the country around

DeKalb for a time, familiarizing himself with the product, then struck out for the mixed cattle and farming country of Texas, accompanied by partner J. P. Warner.[3] Texas appeared ideally suited to barbed wire, and Sanborn and Warner sold a few carloads, but overall their reception was poor, their sales disappointing.

That they would arouse little enthusiasm among stockfarmers could have been anticipated; no one had yet made the great mental leap from the concept of fencing livestock out to that of fencing them in except, perhaps, in the intensively managed pastures of more crowded country. Along the Texas farm line, where corn was raised for food and feed and cattle as a cash crop, livestock were expected to fend for themselves and drift where the grass and water were best. The farther west the line moved, the more arid the country became and the more essential it was that cattle have access to fresh grazing. Few stockfarmers owned much if any of the land they grazed, thus they had neither the right nor the incentive to fence. Those fenced out of customary waterings, in fact, quickly developed an intense dislike for wire. Nor did it sell to the state's "pure" farmers. Located mostly in the eastern counties, these were generally cotton planters, tenant farmers or freeholders scratching a meager living from a piece of dirt worn out long before. All had been ravaged by the recent war and its aftermath. They were too poor to risk experimenting with flimsy-looking wire fencing even if it was guaranteed to protect their crops.

Sanborn and Warner were replaced in Texas by another Glidden relative, a brash and cocky youth named John Warne Gates. Entrepreneur, showman, big dreamer and inveterate gambler, "Bet-A-Million" Gates had the self-confidence to swagger boldly into situations from which more level-headed men might retreat at a high lope. At the age of

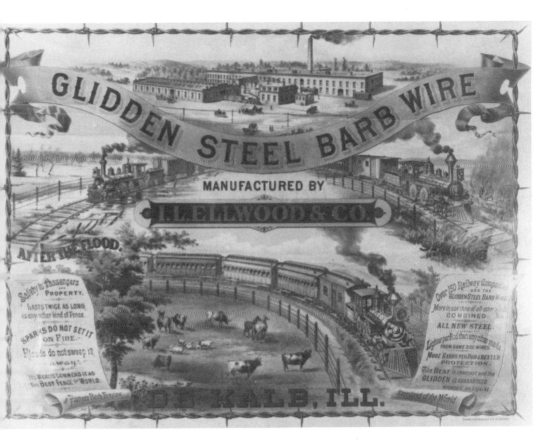

Promotional poster for Ellwood's barbed wire company (Spade Ranches Collection).

twenty-one, Gates left to sell wire to the same Texans who had turned Sanborn and Warner away with satchels full of empty order blanks.[4]

Gates made San Antonio his headquarters, and there he conceived a stunt which would set him on the road to fame and incredible fortune. To prove the strength and effectiveness of barbed wire, he had a corral constructed in one of the town's public plazas and filled with Longhorn cattle. The story has been told and retold so many times that fact and legend are inseparable, but one fact is inarguable: the fence held and Gates proved his point with a public flourish that no amount of sales talk could have matched.

He proved it, moreover, to precisely the right people.

Whether by luck or intuition, Gates' choice of San Antonio placed his dramatic demonstration before the eyes of some of the state's biggest and most influential cowmen, the class of operator who had begun buying land. They led by example, and their acceptance of barbed wire just as tens of thousands of square miles of grazing land were thrown open to Texas herds assured the fortunes of the wire industry.

When J. W. Gates returned in triumph from his Texas foray in 1876, he was characteristically bold in his assumptions about what sort of reward he was due for cracking that huge but reluctant market. By his reckoning he deserved either a full partnership in the company or at least exclusive sales rights for Texas. Ellwood disagreed. The first demand was simply too great, and the second would require violating the sales agreement already held by Sanborn and Warner. Gates had outdone them in their own territory, but Ellwood's loyalty to his first salesmen was not to be questioned. That point was driven home when the Sanborn and Warner contracts expired on the first day of 1877 and Ellwood renewed them.

Gates' response was again characteristic—he split with Ellwood, formed a barbed wire company of his own, and lobbied his Texas contacts to join the mutiny. Suddenly the employer for whom he had peddled so earnestly and convincingly was a greedy wire baron and Gates was the champion who would deliver his customers from monopolistic oppression.[5]

Actually, there were a number of such "champions" out there, some claiming highly questionable prior use patents on armored wire but most content simply to profit by manufacturing others' inventions as long as they could get by with it. Jacob Haish was one of the former, and Gates began as one of the latter.

Had Gates and his "moonshine" crowd been their only class of competitors, Ellwood's Barb Fence Company might have prevailed early and fairly easily. The company at first had no trouble convincing the courts in Missouri to enjoin Gates from making wire in his St. Louis shop. Enforcing the injunction became a comical affair, however, when Gates packed his machinery on a barge and towed it across the Mississippi to the Illinois side just ahead of the process servers. Ellwood was forced to repeat the procedure with Illinois officials, whereupon Gates returned the operation to the Missouri side. His audacity won Gates the support of numerous other clearly illegal wire makers, strengthening his position.[6]

Ellwood's real battle, however, was with Haish and other competitors who claimed to hold legitimate patents. Until these could be individually disproven through costly and tortuous Patent Office fights, nothing could be done to stop that class. And the longer and more complex the quasi-legitimate cases became, the firmer the ground under Gates' feet: until Ellwood, Haish or one of the other claimants could be formally recognized as the true holder of the initial patent on barbed wire, none of them really had the legal standing to deny rights to anyone else. The struggle took a fateful turn in December of 1880 when two Chicago judges ruled for Ellwood's Barb Fence Company in the long-fought legal battle with Jacob Haish. The Haish wire, they decided, infringed on the "foundation" patents belonging to The Barb Fence Company. The crucial ruling held that Haish owed damages for all the wire he had manufactured and sold up to that time.[7] This had the effect of making all the other illegal wire-makers liable for damages as well. Facing such potential devastation, some of the more substantial outfits applied for license from the company and took their licks for past transgressions. Many moonshiners couldn't cover their liabilities and simply closed down. Others, however—Gates among them—preferred to bull their way through. They had been illegal all along and knew it; the Chicago ruling only made it official. The apparent attitude among those who chose to hang and rattle was that the worst they faced was going out of business, and settling with The Barb Fence Company would do that to them anyway. They would stay in business—and make money—as long as they could.

It was 1892 before the patent war—inspired, emboldened and organized by Gates—was finally concluded by a Supreme Court decision recognizing the primacy of the Glidden patent.[8] It had cost Ellwood, his company and his heirs a fortune, and it was a measure of his tenacity and drive that he stayed with the fight, a measure of his humanity and loyalty that his word to Sanborn and Warner precipitated the worst of it. The same qualities are evident in his resumption of both business and private relations with Gates well before all the dust had settled.

By 1891 Gates and Ellwood were allied in a creation of Gates' design known as the Columbia Patent Company.

This combine absorbed other barbed wire manufacturers and metamorphosed again by the waning years of the century into the American Steel & Wire Company. With the old Washburn & Moen as a drawing card, American Steel & Wire in 1901 became a major element of J. Pierpont Morgan's giant United States Steel Corporation.[9] Gates and Ellwood were to partner in a broad range of other investments over the years, Gates naturally playing the role of frontman and promoter, Ellwood remaining backstage as the sober senior partner.

Because of his high visibility, history has tended to credit Gates as the originator of these enterprises, but he himself put a different spin on the story. Speaking to a Chicago reporter on the event of Ellwood's funeral in 1910, Gates fondly described his late mentor, partner, adversary as "a shrewd man who saw his opportunities—just such opportunities as men have every day—and never let one get away from him. No one ever put one over on Col. Ellwood."[10]

The two men remained close personal friends as well as business partners, reportedly never so close as when they were gambling with or against one another. Even in that, however, Gates was the front man and Ellwood the silent partner; his reputation for wagering earned Gates the famous nickname "Bet-a-Million," but Ellwood was apparently a party to many or most of those same wagers. It was said the two once placed hefty bets on which of two raindrops would reach the bottom of a train window first.[11] An Ellwood family story holds that "The Colonel" and Gates once met an obviously displeased Mrs. Ellwood coming downstairs to breakfast at a New York hotel as they were returning to their rooms after an all-night card game. Slipping into the terminology of the horse industry, Gates referred to her nose-high attitude: "checked a might high this mornin', ain't she, Mr. Ellwood?"[12]

For all his travels and successes in the field of high finance and big business, Isaac Ellwood remained devoted to DeKalb. His major dealings might have been on Wall Street, but his heart and home remained in the farmland of Illinois. He supported DeKalb charities large and small, and was instrumental in capturing the Northern Illinois State Normal School for his hometown.[13] There is another family story—with just a touch of light scandal—describing Ellwood's extracurricular efforts to attract the Normal School. It was said to have been unusually dry when officials charged with choosing a site for the teachers' college came to DeKalb, and Ellwood was afraid the low condition of the river through town might provide an unfavorable impression. With his connections he quietly arranged to have the flood gates of an upstream dam opened while the siting committee was in town.[14]

Ellwood also maintained a truly local side to his business, small-scale dealings that at first glance might seem totally out of place alongside his grander ventures. On reflection, however, they offer a clue to the man's success: he was meticulous and, as Gates said, "no one ever put one over on him." Typical of this side of his business are letters from lawyers he had retained to collect on loans. Some of the notes may be presumed to have been given in promise of payment for wire or other goods, but Ellwood was also known as a reliable source of credit for the down-and-out. At least some of the notes may have represented simply personal debts. Whatever their purpose, few amounted to much money in the context of Ellwood's fortunes, but he had agents pursuing their collection as if recovery represented the difference between his survival and bankruptcy.

One such agent writing from Kansas in 1896 expressed genuine regret at his inability to redeem a series of notes. "You got to get somebody else to attend to them for you," the agent wrote. "I can not do any good so I give up."[15] The debts he listed, fifteen in all, ranged from five dollars to a maximum of $56, most falling within a ten to fifteen dollar range. The notes then went to another Kansas attorney, F. Vernon Russell, who reported somewhat better success the following year. One $20 note was owed by a man Russell considered "quite poor but strictly honest and honorable. I think this claim will be all right." It was; a handwritten memo in the margin showed it to have been paid the following year.

Still, there were some even the thorough Russell couldn't "shape up," as he put it. A $25 debt owed by "an old gentleman . . . about ready to die" was "perhaps the worst case we have." Another borrower had "removed to the Territory" still owing $30. The $56 note was held against "a trifling, worthless fellow, indisposed to pay or secure." Russell was "not very hopeful" over the prospects of collecting $15 from "an ornery coon" who "promised to secure it when he put in his next crop," but he was a bit more optimistic about a $26.65 note owed by a couple "reported to me to be worthless and naturally mean" who "had stated that they never intended paying."

Finally, there was a $5 note that Russell and the borrower had negotiated down to $3.25. The lawyer left empty-handed, however, because the debtor lived "30 miles from civilization and I could not make him the change he required." Russell, it appears, had been had and didn't even realize it.[16]

All this was going on while Ellwood and Gates were making million-dollar deals, transforming the Columbia Patent Company into American Steel & Wire, and Ellwood was battling on behalf of DeKalb against other towns interested in the Normal School. Lesser men would have found themselves spread far too thin, but then lesser men would have run aground much earlier in the journey. Many did in that age of robber barons when quick success turned to unbridled greed and men of humble beginnings built huge fortunes only to lose direction and everything else along with it.

"Colonel Ike" Ellwood never lost his direction.

"A lesson might be drawn" from his life, Gates concluded in his eulogy, "the story of a great fortune fairly made by an honest man—no robbing of widows and orphans, no breaking of promises or taking of unfair advantage. I'd rather have had Col. Ellwood's verbal word than the written, sworn statement of many men I know."

Such was the example W. L. Ellwood had been raised to follow. By all accounts he followed it faithfully. W. L. had already taken over much of the family's horse business by the early 1880s, leaving the elder Ellwood more time to devote to his manufacturing and investment interests. In 1885 the son demonstrated a streak of innovativeness that would surface repeatedly in subsequent years; he pioneered the idea of selling his purebred horses with catalogs listing their pedigrees. He was also said to have promoted his stock locally by parading one well-matched pair or another through DeKalb's streets festooned in fancy harness and pulling a red-wheeled surrey. Lovers of horseflesh would follow like the children of mythical Hamlin after the Pied Piper.[17] It was more than business to W. L. He loved horses and horse trading, and pursued them with a devotion that went far beyond any interest in making money.

Acquisition of the Texas property, however, introduced young Ellwood to a new passion that would compete with horses for his attention. Cow country with its wide open spaces, and cow trading with its handshake deals for huge stakes, fired his imagination. His horse-buying trips to Europe, begun at his father's side in the late 1870s and continued for more than a decade afterward, became less frequent in the 1890s as the Renderbrook and Spade ranches consumed more and more of W. L.'s time. The remaining years of the decade were devoted mostly to consolidating existing holdings and developing a ranch routine that would be followed for years to come.

The Ellwoods made at least one significant purchase of additional land during the nineties, however, buying forty-nine sections in Borden County near Gail. Roughly seven miles square, it came to be known simply as the "49 Pasture."[18] It wasn't large in relation to the other Ellwood outfits, nor did it remain a part of the operation for very many years, but the 49 Pasture proved to be a critical addition to the whole.

Located about midway between Renderbrook and the Plains ranch, the new acquisition served as a way stop for Spade cattle on the ten-day drive between ranches. The Ellwood ranches had elected early on to concentrate their cow and calf production at Renderbrook and reserve the Spade mostly for growing out steers. These remained on the Panhandle grass until they were sold as four-year-olds, generally to Kansas buyers who gave them another summer in the Kansas Flinthills before selling them on the Kansas City market or to Cornbelt feedyards.[19]

The real value of the 49 Pasture in those years, however, was its strategic location just north of the old Texas Fever quarantine line. Texas cattle had barely begun moving up the trails to northern markets after the Civil War when farmers and stockmen along the routes discovered that these rangy brutes from the lower country carried a disease from which they themselves were immune but which cut a swath of death through more northerly herds. Even before they learned that the fever was tick-borne they observed that a good freeze would halt its spread. This discovery gave rise to a quarantine line beyond which Texas cattle could not pass until winter. Isolation of the Texas Fever tick as carrier of the disease moved the line back down into Texas itself and led to a systematic dipping program that eventually eradicated the tick in all but the border regions of the state, where Mexican strays still pose a problem.

When the 49 Pasture was purchased, Renderbrook itself lay below the line, and yearling steers leaving there still had to be dipped before moving toward the Spade Ranch on the Plains. The Borden County property provided a place above the line where they could be held long enough to assure that the treatment had been successful before completing the drive. Even if some ticks survived the dip, there were few permanent cattle on the 49 to infest, and cold weather would help with the problem before the next herd came through.[20]

As the 1890s drew to a close, the Spades were poised for a new round of expansion. It began with a divestiture, actually the second of two divestitures.

Colonel I. L. Ellwood had once sold his interest in the barbed wire business to Washburn & Moen, but later bought it back. Still later came his 1891 alliance with J. W. Gates in the Columbia Patent Company and the various incarnations that followed.[21] By the late nineties, however, the wire industry was losing its allure for Colonel Ellwood. It had made him wealthy beyond any dreams the DeKalb hardware merchant could have had, but he was well into his sixth decade. He had nursed barbed wire through its formative years, weathered the moonshine manufacturer wars and the court battles, and watched the industry mature as countless thousands of miles of his product laced the nation with cheap, durable and effective fencing. Now the industry he had established no longer needed his guidance. Perhaps even more important, his elder son, W. L., had his own interests firmly anchored elsewhere. Ellwood's younger son, Perry, was still in school, and remaining Ellwood offspring were daughters Harriet May, Mary Patience and Jessie Hoyt. It was considered unthinkable at the time that the business world should appeal to women.

With yet another of the Gates consolidations and reorganizations underway in 1898, Ellwood sold his interests for the second and final time.[22] This provided an influx of fresh capital and some free time in which to consider ways to invest it. It didn't require much soul-searching on the part of the Ellwoods to figure out where to put part of it.

Expansion

5

$\large{A}$S they had first done nearly ten years before, Isaac and W. L. Ellwood again took the train together for Texas. The trip was begun under the auspices of a vacation for the father, presumably a well-earned one after what must have been a draining experience closing out a major chapter of his life. The focus quickly shifted, however. Within days after his arrival on the Plains, Colonel Ellwood had his eye on another piece of land. Roughly 45,000 acres contiguous to the Spade had gone unstocked for several years. Once known as the "south pasture" of the Snyder Brothers outfit, this tract had sold for $25,000 in a sheriff's auction to a group from Michigan and Illinois. Ellwood deduced from the lack of grazing activity that the owners had bought the land strictly for investment purposes rather than to ranch it, and back to DeKalb he went to begin negotiations for its purchase. It took until April of 1902 to get it done and then only at a hefty $3 per acre, but the old Snyder holdings were finally rejoined and the Spade boasted nearly 174,000 acres.[1]

The expansion didn't stop there.[2]

With the addition of the south Snyder pasture, W. L.'s Texas responsibilities had increased once again. More fencing, more improvements and fresh country to stock required so much of his time that he was literally living on the Spade and Renderbrook. Instead of trips to Texas, he was now making trips home, and these became fewer all the time. This close and constant proximity to the ranch country brought more familiarity with the dealings going on around the Plains ranch, and he began to hear of more opportunities for land purchases. Adjoining the Spade on the south were about 17,500 acres of one-time Jones County school lands then owned by an H. A. Pierce. Like the south Snyder, this outfit was being offered at $3 an acre. With his father's approval, W. L. met Pierce's price on October 17, 1904, and the Spade swelled to almost 191,000 acres.

More land hit the market the following year, and once again the Ellwoods were interested. The total acreage was about 73,000, held by various parties including Pierce, and most of this expanse, like those before, abutted on the southern boundaries of the Spade. The largest portion was the old Lake Tomb Cattle Company, also known as the Nunn Ranch. It covered 115 sections of which only about fifteen were deeded, the remainder still held by the state as Wichita, Wilbarger and Donley County school lands. It was a big chunk to bite off, and having essentially established the local market at $3 per acre with their previous purchases, the Ellwoods had a good idea what it would cost them. Colonel Ike couldn't bring himself to take that deep a plunge without personal investigation, so once again he took a Texas "vacation." Once on the ground, he found no surprises, and he authorized the purchase of the hundred sections of school land. The price, as before, was $3.

The only fly in the ointment was the four-section block held by Pierce, with whom they had dealt on the Jones

County land the previous year. This tract lay well within the new Spade range since its expansion by the other purchases, and the significance of that location wasn't lost on Pierce.

Colonel Ellwood had returned to Illinois after approving the Lake Tomb deal, leaving W. L. to negotiate on the outstanding four sections. He didn't have much room for negotiation. Pierce had him over a barrel and knew it; he pegged his price at $4.50 an acre, take it or leave it. W. L. swallowed hard, accepted Pierce's terms and drew a draft on his father for the total. Judge R. C. Hopping's version of the elder Ellwood's reaction has the ring of truth to it: "You are going to break me buying that Texas land," he quoted Ike as saying, followed "almost in the same sentence" by an order to investigate yet another purchase.

A remaining tract of four leagues would roughly square up the perimeter of the Spade and give the Plains ranch a total of about 265,000 acres. Formerly Howard County school land, it was then held by a Charles E. Leonard of Missouri. Hopping noted nothing particularly unique about the land or improvements, if any, on the range offered by Leonard. The Missourian, however, either thought he had something special or figured the Ellwoods would see it that way. Like Pierce, he wasn't content with the $3 going rate. Unlike Pierce, even $4.50 didn't suit him. The Ellwoods finally closed the deal on July 7, 1906, for $5.65 per acre.

The purchase stretched the Spade into a rectangle roughly forty-eight miles long by about eight to twelve miles wide, giving Colonel Ellwood approximately 395,000 acres of Texas land including Renderbrook. In three short decades the Illinois storekeeper had built and sold one empire, and replaced it with a second of a far different sort.

But land alone doesn't make a ranch. It must have capable men to handle the livestock and capable foremen to

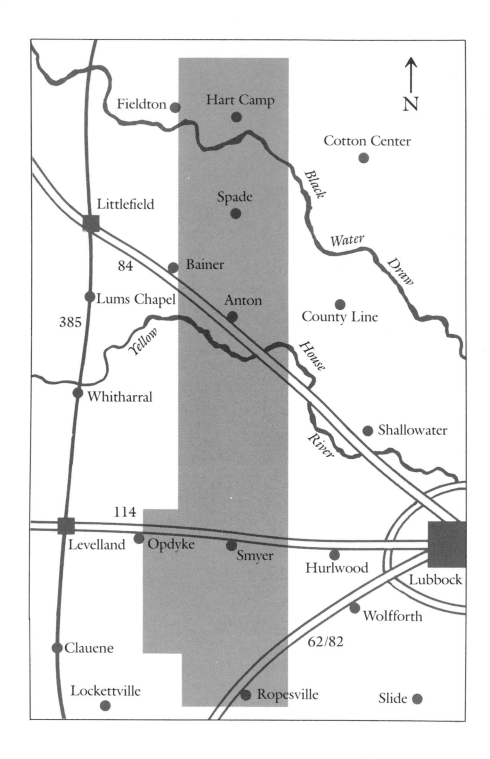

SPADE RANCH

direct the men. The Spades were blessed with both from the beginning. In Uncle Dick Arnett the Ellwoods found not only a seasoned veteran of range and trail, but a man who was able to adapt the lessons of that wild and unfenced era to the changing demands of more settled ranching. A successful cowhunter or trailboss had to know how to read the land—to take the measure of unfamiliar country from such clues as its drainages, the depth of soil exposed in cliff faces and washouts, and the abundance and variety of its vegetation and wild game. Too many men, seeing virgin West Texas range for the first time during a brief period of uncommonly abundant rainfall, had overestimated its carrying capacity. Others of an opposite bent had labeled some of the same land "desert" because it lacked the forests and running streams that had been their only previous experience.

Men in Arnett's line of work had to concern themselves with reality rather than the extremes of either boosterism or condemnation. Hunting wild cows or trailing a herd, they learned to locate fuel and shelter, water and grass, and they learned to recognize the signs that revealed whether an abundance of the latter two necessities was dependable or temporary. It was this knowledge the Ellwoods drew on when they asked Arnett to help them size up the Snyders' Panhandle outfit in 1891, and it was the benefit of his experience with cattle and men they sought when they put him in charge of both that operation and Renderbrook.

It may have been Arnett who steered the two ranches toward their different but complementary roles, Renderbrook that of a cow and calf outfit, and the Spade a growing range for steers the other ranch produced. He had the cow sense, at least, to realize that yearling and older steers could take the cold winters of the open Panhandle with its scarcity of natural shelter better than cows and young calves.

If the Ellwoods had any initial qualms about Arnett's loyalties in the potentially touchy matter of advising his new employers on the purchase of ranchland from his old employers, those concerns must have evaporated quickly. Along with his other cowman traits, Arnett carried a strong streak of fidelity to the outfit he worked for. He treated Spade concerns as he would his own, and that was no-where more evident than in his almost legendary devotion to pinching pennies. Hopping relates that cooks with the wagons were instructed to waste "no part of a beef when killed."[3] Campfires at the Spade wagons during Arnett's tenure had a perennial pot of son-of-a-gun stew on the coals, the meat ingredient made up chiefly of hearts, livers and other organs. The concoction went back on the fire day after day, camp after camp, until it was gone.

Spade wagons were known for feeding well if somewhat monotonously. Desserts such as dutch-oven cobblers from canned peaches, however, were an extravagance Arnett seldom allowed, but he did keep his crews in mind. On one visit to a camp, foreman Arnett left his horse-drawn hack a respectful distance from the chowline, as was the custom to avoid stirring up dust around the food. When he reached the chuckwagon he pointed back toward the rig. "I brought some fruit," he said, "if some of you boys would like to go get it." The announcement sparked a jingling stampede of spurred boots, followed by the much more subdued return of several cowboys with a can or two each of stewed tomatoes.[4]

Uncle Dick Arnett's management was considered exem-plary in all respects. In addition to bringing the neophyte Ellwoods along as large-scale cowmen, he presided over the transformation of Renderbrook and the Spade from es-sentially open range outfits to fully fenced ranches while learning the ropes of that new and complex form of the business himself. All the while he had to contend with a growing operation and all the demands such an expansion made on his skills and organizational ability. But Arnett's contributions outlasted even his own tenure. In hiring Uncle Dick in 1891, Isaac and W. L. Ellwood secured for their enterprise, probably unwittingly, a continuity of management that would carry it well into the twentieth century and lay the foundation for successive generations of employees. Dick Arnett, Jr., known as "Little Dick," signed on as a horse wrangler when his father brought the family to Renderbrook. Literally born into the cowboying profession, he was considered experienced enough at his craft to take over management of the North Spade division by the time Frank Norfleet departed in 1904.[5]

The next member of the Arnett clan to go to work for the Ellwoods was nephew Wylie Daniel Arnett, known to everyone as Tom. (Nicknames were popular in the family and were sometimes carried over and adopted by following generations as given names. W. D. "Tom" Arnett's grandson was christened Tom, III, and Little Dick eventually became Uncle Dick to a later generation, the "Little" appellation passing on to his own son. How David Nathan senior ever became "Dick" is unclear, as is the transformation from Wylie Daniel to Tom.)

Tom Arnett's career with the Spades began in 1906 and was to span several decades.[6] He started at Renderbrook, working out of first one camp and then another. The camp system was common on most large ranches at the time, following from the open-range practice of stationing cowboys along an outfit's perimeters to keep cattle thrown back onto the proper range. The line riders' principal focus shifted somewhat with the coming of fences, but there were bogs to check in season, health problems to keep an eye on, and the fences to ride and maintain. During the warm

Uncle Dick Arnett and his family (above) about 1900 (Southwest Collection, Texas Tech University). *Below, Spade cowboys in front of the chuckwagon* (Southwest Collection, Texas Tech University).

months, doctoring for screwworms tended to monopolize the cowboys' time. Before pickups and horse trailers became commonplace, these activities required men to be stationed more or less permanently at strategically located points; there simply weren't enough hours in the day to ride horseback from headquarters to the more distant locations, do the work that needed doing, then drag back in bone-weary on an equally exhausted mount.

With a camp job came responsibility. A green cowboy on a wagon crew had plenty of other men around him to clean up any messes he made. He either learned from his mistakes and made a hand or was given his time. There were usually enough eyes on him to minimize the consequences of inexperience, poor judgement or slack behavior. A camp man, on the other hand, might be on his own for weeks at a stretch, enough time for minor errors to grow into large scale wrecks. Thus a camp assignment was a vote of confidence, seldom bestowed lightly. Tom Arnett held a succession of them. More than likely the cycle of assignments tracked his increasing level of experience, beginning at a post where his duties may have been fairly limited and culminating at whatever camp posed the greatest challenge at the time.

The years 1907 and 1908 saw two more Arnetts added to the Spade payroll. Tom's brother, Albert Henry "George" Arnett, replaced Little Dick as manager of the North Spade in 1908, and Cullen Bascomb "Bass" Arnett took over for Renderbrook's departing wagonboss, Sam Moreland, that fall.' Moreland was Uncle Dick's brother-in-law, and Bass Arnett had had about a year of cowboying under him.

By that time, W. L. Ellwood's immersion in the Texas cattle business had become total. In addition to his efforts on behalf of the family interests he was carrying on an almost constant stream of land and cattle deals in his own

"Spade Peelers," (above) fall 1907, at Colorado City. Left to right, Otto Jones, cook Jim Smith (in wagon), horse wranglers Bill Ledbetter and Ovid Creighton, trail boss Fred Rodway, Bass Arnett, and brothers Walter, Ed and Robert Arnold (Southwest Collection, Texas Tech University). Below, W. D. "Tom" Arnett, 1929 (Southwest Collection, Texas Tech University).

name. Most of these were partnership ventures, and one of those partners was George Arnett.

Hopping notes that W. L. was a man "of a restless disposition" who "did not like to concentrate on complicated problems."[8] Ordinarily that might be a ruinous personality trait for an individual with Ellwood's apparent addiction to cattle trading, but he also appears to have been an excellent judge of character. His approach was to choose capable partners who could and would attend to the details that bored him, then back them to the hilt financially.

In 1911, W. L. relieved George Arnett of day-to-day management of the North Spade, moving him to an office in Lubbock, which Hopping explained was "more centrally located" for his new assignment, overseeing both divisions of the Plains ranch. The change doubtless left Arnett freer to keep an eye on their various outside deals as well. Tom Arnett moved into his brother's former post at the North Spade, where he would remain for another decade and a half. Bass Arnett, meanwhile, had taken over as resident manager of the South Spade the year before. The Arnett family had clearly put its management stamp on the Ellwood operation.[9]

Uncle Dick's oldest son, Sam, apparently never worked for the Spades, but his association with the Ellwoods was no less close.[10] The Arnetts' Scissors Ranch sold just after the turn of the century, and Sam Arnett struck out on his own, leasing fifty-five sections from the Hat Ranch in Andrews County. This was a short-term deal, and by the summer of 1901 he was operating another leased outfit in the vicinity of Plainview. Within months he had moved 1200 cows onto the North Spade's Hart's Camp pasture in Lamb and Hale counties.

Sam Arnett wintered his herd there and by spring was embroiled in both a lice outbreak and a price slump. Be-

tween them, they threatened to do him in, but Colonel
Ellwood came to the rescue. Ellwood took the steer end of
Arnett's cattle for $20 a head, a $3 premium on the weak
market at the time, and wrote off the winter pasture bill in
the bargain. Arnett, in turn, vacated the lease to make way
for Spade cattle, relocating a few miles north on Running
Water Draw.

When the Ellwoods bought the Lake Tomb-Nunn Ranch
outfit in early 1905, Sam Arnett was part of the deal. He
took over management with a working interest in the 115
section tract, which Colonel Ike dubbed the "Poor Boy Cattle Company." It was apparently Sam and W. L.'s baby,
each taking half interest in about 4000 head of cattle and
saddle horses and, presumably, fifteen sections of deeded
land. The elder Ellwood leased them twelve leagues of
former school land he had retained to block with the Spade,
and apparently financed the overall operation. Hopping
says Sam Arnett's note to I. L. Ellwood was "a little more
than $100,000," a serious chunk of money for that day and
time. It came to look more serious still a couple of years
later when another in the nation's series of financial panics
set in. Hopping relates that bank customers were limited to
withdrawals of no more than $5 per day of their own
money. A recurring irony at such times is that the failures
of many become opportunities for a few, and the 1907 panic
was Sam Arnett's turn. Isaac Ellwood's wealth was not all
in banks with someone else's hand on the key; some of it
was liquid, and Arnett's close relationship provided him
access to a little of the flow in case of need.

Arnett found his need in cheap cattle, their prices forced
to rock-bottom by the financial collapse. He wasn't the only
one who knew prices would recover along with the econ-
omy, but he was one of the few in a position to own cattle
when the turnaround came. While others helplessly

watched the bargains go by, unable to get their hands on the money to take advantage of them, Sam Arnett picked up a telephone and placed a call to DeKalb, Illinois. With $50,000 cash, he told Colonel Ellwood, he could retire his debt in full within six months. It was an ambitious promise, but Arnett knew his business. He also knew his friend; Ellwood wired him $5000 more than he asked for.

The precious capital in hand, Sam Arnett was in a position to sit back and let the sellers come to him. They did just that, and within a few months the market recovered as it always had. By the spring of 1908, just as he had predicted, Arnett "cleared up" his entire debt to the Colonel. His half of the Nunn Ranch operation was in the black, thanks to his own shrewd eye for trading and the faith of the man from DeKalb.

With his half interest now truly his own, Arnett's foothold on the cow business was secure enough to allow him to branch out. He and W. L. Ellwood hit on the idea of buying cattle from below the tick line, cleaning them up, then selling them at a profit to buyers above the quarantine. To make that project work properly, they needed strategically located land somewhere in the clean area but near the line like the Spades' 49 Pasture. There was either nothing available, or nothing as suitable for their purposes as the 49, so Arnett and W. L. approached Isaac Ellwood about the Spade property itself. The Colonel must have given the matter serious thought, considering the 49's importance to his own program. Still, the role his son and young Arnett had in mind for the tract would more fully utilize it. He accepted their proposition in the end, but apparently with provisions for some continued use by Renderbrook; Hopping put the sale of the 49 to Sam and W. L. in 1908, but other accounts note that Renderbrook steers continued to pasture there until 1910–1911, when the property finally sold to outside interests.

One of those outside interests was Rube Clayton, who at about that same time joined Arnett and W. L. in another ranch purchase. Between them, the trio bought the Clabber Hill and C ranches in Andrews County. Clabber Hill contained 135 sections, the C Ranch a hundred sections. Clayton sold his share in the two outfits to Arnett and Ellwood in the early 1920s, and Arnett bought out Ellwood's part of the Clabber Hill Ranch in 1931. It eventually sold, but the Clabber Hill name carried over to another ranch that remains in Arnett family hands today.

The Ellwood-Arnett partnership reached beyond ranches and cows, culminating in 1931 in the joint purchase of near-total ownership of the Citizens' National Bank of Lubbock. Hopping put the figure at ninety-seven percent of the stock, purchased in a block from France Baker. Arnett initially took controlling interest with fifty-one percent against Ellwood's forty-six, and assumed the presidency.

I. L. Ellwood could not have foreseen such a close relationship developing between the two families when he sought out Uncle Dick Arnett as a manager in 1891, and he didn't live to see its full flowering. Two days after Independence Day in 1910, Isaac Ellwood's wife of fifty-three years died at their home in DeKalb.[11] Her passing literally took the heart out of him, and within days he began putting his own affairs in final order. He consulted with his children on the disposition of the vast estate he would leave behind, and his will followed their wishes as closely as possible. As executors he named sons W. L. and Perry Ellwood, along with his long-time secretary, A. W. Fisk.

Six weeks after losing his wife, Colonel I. L. Ellwood breathed his last.[12] It was September 11, 1910, one month and one day past his seventy-seventh birthday. Hopping records that the memorial service in DeKalb's Armory Theatre drew 3000 people, and an account in the *Chicago Sunday*

Tribune of September 18, 1910, mentions a "special train" reserved "to take guests to and from the funeral."[13]

The Colonel's will, filed for probate on September 27, specified that his daughters were to receive cash for their interests in the huge Ellwood Estate, sons W. L. and Perry the ranches and other real estate. Perry Ellwood also succeeded his father as president of the First National Bank of DeKalb, a position that commanded his presence and left W. L. to look after their Texas interests essentially alone. W. L. was also chief executor of the estate, with all the responsibilities that implied. A. W. Fisk's nearly thirty years of service as I. L.'s personal secretary, accountant and legal advisor was doubtless put to good use in relieving some of the pressure on the late Ellwood's elder son, but there were still myriad details only W. L. could attend to.[14]

That situation probably played a large part in the shuffling of management back in Texas the following year which moved George Arnett to Lubbock and shifted his brother Tom from Renderbrook to the North Spade.

It may also be that W. L. was looking ahead to the next major change confronting the ranch operation—replacing Uncle Dick Arnett. Uncle Dick had put in a busy half century since his brief service with the Texas Rangers in 1869. He had trailed cattle to Wyoming, bossed open-range outfits for the Snyder brothers, established a ranch of his own, and for two decades had overseen the growth of the Spade brand for the Ellwoods. With his sons grown, trained and well situated, he was ready to retire and shed some of the responsibilities that had swelled with the Spade operation. Uncle Dick left Renderbrook in the spring of 1912, driving a new buggy and team chosen by George and provided by the ranch as a parting gift.[15] His place at Renderbrook was taken by a young cowboy he'd hired five years before and with whose father he had cowhunted long, long years previous.

Cowmen, Cattle and Horseflesh

6

UNCLE DICK ARNETT was with the wagon dipping cattle one hot mid-August day in 1907 when tall, lanky Otto Jones rode up in search of a job. Jones was eighteen years old, cowboying in the summer between school terms. He had just finished a couple of months of work for George McEntire's U Ranch west of Sterling City and was headed back in the general direction of Nolan County, where his father, W. D. "Black Bill" Jones, was foreman of the H Triangle Bar near Maryneal.[1]

The elder Jones, remembering the cowhunting partner of his youth, had told his son to keep Uncle Dick in mind if he was ever in need of a job. With a few weeks of summer left and Renderbrook on his way, Otto gave it a shot. As was common among young single cowboys, Jones carried most of his worldly possessions with him in his bedroll. Included was his one good suit, which on this particular day he chose to wear to give it an airing. Riding up to the wagon thus attired, he unwittingly became part of a practical joke.

Second wagonboss Fred Rodway pointed out the suited rider to the horse jingler as W. L. Ellwood. Rodway knew better but the green puncher didn't, and when Rodway told him to hurry out and hold "Mr. Ellwood's" horse, the jingler quickly complied. Jones was impressed at the hospitality the Renderbrook outfit extended toward a job-hunter like himself, and the victim of the joke was so impressed at meeting a wealthy ranch "owner" that he patiently stood and held the horse while Jones ate at the wagon and had his conference with Arnett. He was offered $25 a month, a good wage for the time but not extravagant. And Arnett also offered him something of a challenge.

"The man that stays is the man that wins," Arnett said, and Jones never forgot it. He accepted both the wage and the challenge. In the end he stayed nearly sixty years, and after his retirement in 1966 continued to live on at Renderbrook another three years before moving into Colorado City. Even then he maintained his ties, driving a Spade car out to the ranch every few days and keeping tabs for several more years.

All that was in the future, however. First Jones had to make a hand, and he began with the dipping crew. That particular day's dipping job involved more cows than usual. It would be several years before Renderbrook began a serious effort to clean up its resident herd, but a drouth had come to the country as it often had before and would again, and the outfit was moving some of its cows north to the Spade.

The law in those days specified that cattle be dipped twice before moving into clean country, and general practice at Renderbrook was to move out right after the second trip through the vat. This held down any likelihood of reinfestation, but it also left the cattle susceptible to overheating from the nicotine sulphate solution used in the dip. As

Otto Jones about 1912 (Southwest Collection, Texas Tech University).

a result, most drives from Renderbrook to the 49 Pasture were made at a deliberately slow pace. The herds were moved during the cool morning hours, rested during the heat of the day, then driven again well into the evening.

It was a four-day drive to the 49, and Jones would make many more after that first one. He recalled in later years that herds leaving Renderbrook were trailed along fenced county lanes the first several miles. Once they reached the Bush & Tillar Ranch where pastures were larger, they could spread out a bit. That pattern prevailed for many years, though the country was gradually fenced up into smaller chunks which complicated movement.

Jones quickly settled into the routine at Renderbrook and sort of "forgot" about his schooling. The next spring he began driving yearling steers to the 49, where they were left to grow out. The trail crew would then put together a herd of two-year-olds from the previous spring's drive and carry them on to the Spade. Jones served under wagonboss Bass Arnett for just over a year, beginning in the fall of 1908.

One drive during that period proved that Uncle Dick Arnett's penchant for pinching pennies was a family trait. It occurred in the spring of 1908, and was described in two slightly different accounts as being a drive from Renderbrook to the Spade rather than one of the shorter trips to the 49 Pasture.[2] This indicates it was a cow drive, which in turn suggests the drouth was still on in the Renderbrook country. W. L.'s daughter Jessie, known to everyone as Jean, was down from DeKalb for a visit, and begged her parents to let her make the drive. If Arnett would give her a mount of horses, she told them, she would make a hand.

This wasn't the sort of activity in which proper young ladies were supposed to be engaged, at least by Illinois standards. Her mother had distinct reservations. It's likely W. L. had a few doubts of his own, but his love for the ranch and ranch life probably tempered them. And it was his enthusiasm, after all, that had rubbed off on his girls. Together Jean and her father worked out a deal—if Mrs. Bass Arnett would travel along to keep an eye on her, the young ranch heiress could go. The one hitch was the tender age of the Arnetts' young son, Howell, which confined Mrs. Arnett to the ranch hack. Young Mary Arnett and one of her girlfriends from Colorado City volunteered to help out, and the three girls and Mrs. Arnett hit the trail with the cowboys and the herd.

A thunderstorm blew up the second night, providing Jean Ellwood with just the excitement she had sought. Astride a good night horse, she was in the saddle until daylight. There was apparently no serious stampede and no cattle lost in the long night of guarded drifting, but Jean was wet to the bone, chilled and tired. She told her daughter Marion in later years that she must have looked a little peaked in the daylight, because Bass Arnett rode off to a nearby ranch and returned with an egg to bolster her strength. True to the family's frugal nature, "He didn't bring eggs for everyone, just one egg for Mom."

The end of the drive was celebrated back at Renderbrook with what became known as the "Bass Arnett Ball," a cowboy dance in the grand tradition. Hopping goes into considerable detail about the preparations, from floor scrubbing to pie baking and "doughnuts by the tubsful," all of which would make it sound a bit more like it should have been called the Mrs. Bass Arnett Ball.[3]

Otto Jones was enough at home at Renderbrook by the time of the dance that W. L. Ellwood ribbed him like he would a member of the family. Jones was known as quite a fiddler, but that night he didn't play, and W. L. took great delight in telling the other cowboys—in Jones' presence—just why that was. Otto had been in the bunkhouse playing his fiddle all alone, Ellwood explained, chewing tobacco and spitting in the fireplace, "in a deep study" over some weighty matter, "when in the twinkling of an eye" the distracted young cowboy "uncrossed his knee, spit his tobacco in the middle of the bed and threw his fiddle in the fire."

That easy relationship between Jones and Ellwood grew. When Bass Arnett moved to the South Spade as manager in 1910, Jones took his place as wagonboss at Renderbrook. Two years later, when Uncle Dick retired, Otto Jones was named Renderbrook's manager. He was just twenty-three years old.[4]

His first major task as manager began within a couple of years as the tick cleanup started in earnest on Renderbrook. Jones later termed that operation the biggest single job of his career. To accomplish it required dipping all cattle every twenty-one days to break the tick's life cycle. With about 6000 mother cows on Renderbrook, it was inevitable that some would be missed just about every round, allowing some ticks to complete their cycles and reproduce. Facing this reality, Uncle Dick had predicted that the job would never be completed, and as a result it wasn't a high priority during his long years as manager. Renderbrook had dipping vats at least as early as 1901, but they were used mainly for cattle destined to move north across the tick line. The only members of the permanent mother herd dipped in those days were the ones that were handy when other cattle were going through the vats.

Uncle Dick's pessimism about the cleanup may have stemmed from his experience with the 49 Pasture, where the job was done a few years earlier. The odds were much better there because most of the cattle were transient or at best semi-permanent, and every head of Spade stock came freshly dipped to begin with. In addition, the 49 was only a

fraction the size of Renderbrook. It was a tall order, nevertheless, greatly complicated by the cattle of a handful of
nesters who held small parcels of land within its borders.
W. L. had finally broken down and told Arnett to buy up all
the nester stock, even dead ones if necessary, to remove
those internal sources of reinfestation. That tactic must
have proven expensive as some of the small-holders, seeing
the Spades' determination, realized their strong positions
in such a seller's market.[5]

In the end, W. L. had to buy the nesters' land as well, but
the 49 Pasture was eventually free of fever ticks. Doing the
same on Renderbrook became almost a full-time job. The
wagon crew left headquarters in April as the weather began
warming up, and it stayed out until December, well after
the first hard frosts. Often Jones was unable to stick to the
prescribed twenty-one-day dipping interval, and the periods stretched to as long as thirty days.

That was better than no dipping at all, but it wasn't good
enough. Combined with the cows that managed to evade
the cowboys off and on, the occasional delays allowed a
reservoir of ticks to remain. It was beginning to look as if
Uncle Dick had been right about the futility of the Renderbrook cleanup effort; Jones had been fighting ticks with
determination since 1914, and three years later the ticks still
had the upper hand.

Then nature intervened. As so often happened, the bless-
ing was difficult to recognize at first, because it came
cloaked in the form of the severe 1916–1918 drouth.

Renderbrook grass dried, then burned, and finally disappeared. Old cows grew gaunt and weak, and young
cows aged before their time. Still the rains wouldn't come.
As the situation deteriorated, the outfit began loosening up
on numbers. The better cows went to the Spade, others to
the packer, until eventually Renderbrook was down to

A Spade cowboy mounts up at the chuckwagon camp for work on the plains (Southwest Collection, Texas Tech University).

about 1500 head, a fourth of what it had carried before the drouth began.

That reduction, it turned out, was just what Jones needed to turn the corner on the fever ticks. His success rate on dipping roundups improved with far fewer cows to account for, and he began rotating the herd from pasture to pasture. That in itself gave him a powerful new weapon; without cows to feed on, a vacated pasture's entire hatch of ticks would starve before it could mature and lay eggs for the next hatch. By the time the drouth was over, so was Renderbrook's long battle with fever ticks. "Otto," Ellwood told Jones, "you wore out 5000 cows, but I believe you got those ticks."[6]

It was the end of an era for the Spades, and the beginning of another one. The drawdown in cow numbers forced by the drouth also led indirectly to a change in another long-standing aspect of life on the Ellwood ranches. In 1919 a cryptic notation in one of the little pocket daybooks Otto Jones carried throughout his life told the story without a wasted word: "changed Shorthorns to Herefords."[7]

The Spades had run Shorthorns, known in the early days by their older name of Durhams, since that first herd they purchased from J. F. Evans in 1889. By the early years of the new century, however, Herefords had caught on in popularity because they were supposed to be "hardier." At least that's what the *Hereford Journal* said, and Jones told an interviewer that "some of the smart boys" had begun reading the *Journal*.[8]

Once it started, the Spades' changeover to Herefords was fairly rapid. It apparently began with the Plains ranch replacing Shorthorn bulls with whitefaces during the drouth. The search for hardiness to counter the poor conditions of the time probably spurred that switch. When the rains returned to Renderbrook, so did the cows, but by then the older ones were gone, and it was mostly half-Hereford heifers that came back down from the Spade. These were two year-olds for the most part, with good Hereford markings. The Ellwoods had always been color-conscious, even with their Shorthorns, and cut out for beef the mottle-faced and lineback heifers, leaving a straight red herd that was able to make the transition to Hereford coloration even before they were full blood.[9] Jones' 1919 notation probably refers to the day Renderbrook itself turned out Hereford bulls in place of Shorthorns, marking the final stage in the breed change. A common ratio at that time was six bulls to a hundred cows.[10]

One of the more colorful elements of ranch life in the early days was the chuckwagon camp, and the heaviest dash of color more often than not was supplied by the cook. From the inception of the chuckwagon during trail driving days following the Civil War, cooks had a reputation as characters, and it was often a well-earned reputation. The camp was their domain, and they ruled it without question. Even the wagonboss deferred to the cook; if the situation became intolerable the boss might fire him, but short of that the cook ran the camp.

Otto Jones in later years set down his recollections of some of the early Renderbrook cooks,[11] beginning with Jim Smith, who reigned over the wagon in 1907 when Jones signed on. Smith, he recalled, was noted for his weather forecasts. The wagon in those days was a traveling repository for the entire crew, carrying not only cooking equipment and foodstocks, but bedrolls, extra clothing, tools and spare gear. For most cowboys, that list included a slicker. Rainwear might not often be needed in arid West Texas, but it eased the discomfort of those times when the sky opened up on men horseback.

Many times the sky just threatened, and that was when

Smith's forecasts were most valued. Jones pointed out that the added weight of a heavy slicker tied behind the saddle "didn't help a sore-backed horse," so cowboys preferred not to carry them if they weren't going to be needed. When a storm looked likely, they would seek Smith's advice before leaving the wagon in the morning. "He very seldom missed," Jones said.

A black cook named Lee Proctor also ran the Renderbrook wagon for a time, and it was his habit to "announce his bill of fare" at each meal, using colorful titles for the various dishes. One was "spotted pup," a dessert made with rice and raisins and seasoned with a dash of cinnamon. Cold biscuits sometimes replaced the rice, and Proctor was fond of calling it "French dish" on occasion, "to make it more mysterious." Proctor called plain rice "swampseed" or "moonshine," and Jones recalled other cooks referring to rice as "John Chinaman." Proctor's name for a pot of combined leftovers was "clean up the kitchen," and sometimes "homogenous mass."

Another Proctor dish was made by frying strips of sourdough in a dutch oven of hot fat. He called it "houn' ears" or "whirlups." A sweetened version similar to doughnuts was known as "bearsign," most likely an allusion to its appearance rather than its taste. "Pooch" was an old favorite made of cold biscuits and canned tomatoes, and Proctor called frijoles either Mexican or Pecos "strawberries" or, more irreverently, "prairie whistle." He made a boiled pudding he called "lumpy Dick," and his flour gravy was billed as "immigrant butter" or "Texas butter."

Proctor's name for pancakes was "splatter dabs" and sometimes "saddle blankets." He sometimes fried up a thick version of potato chips known by the old name of "Saratoga chips." Hearing him announce that treat, Jones remembered, "really made you prick up your ears." Some of his staples were less admired, or at least they didn't wear well after repeated servings. Jones recalled a time when Proctor made up a two-gallon batch of "spotted pup" before the wagon left headquarters. "We done very well with the first gallon," he wrote, but boredom set in before the second half was consumed. Otto's brother, Fred Jones, "accidently on purpose" knocked the crock off the chuckwagon lid, spilling the remainder.

"Look here, Proc," Otto quoted him as saying, "darn my carelessness, I've ruined the spotted pup."

"That's alright, Mr. Fred," Proctor answered, "I'll cook some more tomorrow."

And he did.

It was essential that a chuckwagon cook know how to improvise when supplies ran short, because it was no small matter to restock out on the range. Once, Jones recorded, a Renderbrook cook had already committed a precious gallon can of apples to a cobbler when he discovered there was no more cinammon in the chuckbox. Not to be stymied by a little detail like that, the cook substituted a generous dose of mint-flavored Copenhagen snuff. Jones pronounced it "pretty good."

Another cook was Walter "Coosey" Jackson, "Coosey" being an Anglicized corruption of the Spanish *cocinero*, meaning cook. Jackson was known to chide the cowboys for their "easy" jobs. "Shucks, fellows, I forgot to bring ya'll any chairs," he told one crew at a roundup, then added, "Aw, well, you cowboys git to set down all the time anyway."[12]

Jones said "oldtime" black cook Perry Bracey called salt pork "Kansas City fish." Bracey's cooking had such a reputation that Colonel Ellwood retained him to cook for his family when they were at Renderbrook. He did it camp

Renderbrook headquarters (above) as they appeared in 1915. Below, "South Spade" headquarters (both from Southwest Collection, Texas Tech University).

style, though, using a chuckwagon parked out behind the White House.

Bracey's private cooking earned him $1.50 a day in 1907, compared to the usual $30 a month paid for camp cooks and the $25 wage of a good cowboy. Second wagonboss Fred Rodway was paid $35, but the deal required him to pay fifteen cents per meal at the wagon, whereas board was included in the wages of the single boys. This arrangement most likely reflected the fact that Rodway was married and generally ate at his own table rather than at the bunkhouse with the single hands. He was thus entitled to somewhat more pay in lieu of the meals provided for the others. When he was with the wagon, however, three meals a day for thirty days could leave him taking home less than the men under him, and in those days the wagon was out for months at a stretch. Sam Moreland, the wagonboss when Jones arrived, earned $45 a month, and Uncle Dick, as general manager, commanded the then-princely sum of $208.33. The unusual precision of that figure is unexplained.

There was no workers' compensation then—literally. The ranch might pay the doctor bills for a cowboy injured in the line of duty, but one hurt fooling around was on his own. In addition, his wages were docked for whatever time he was off the job recuperating. Otto Jones learned that the hard way in June of 1908.

He was off visiting his brother Fred, who had yet to join the Renderbrook payroll, and climbed aboard a bronc to "demonstrate how it was done on the Spade Ranch." The bronc was just as determined to demonstrate his own abilities, and Jones hit the ground hard, breaking his collarbone. "Uncle Dick didn't fail to dock a puncher if he didn't work," Jones recalled later. "His motto was 'no work, no pay.'"[13]

It cost Otto two weeks' wages, which shows how fast such an injury can mend when it has to. It may also go a long way toward explaining the long legacy of crooked legs, knocked-down hips and other skeletal warpage that cowboys of the era carried into their golden years as a result of fractures that were seldom given the time or attention to mend properly.

A single cowboy's material needs were fairly modest at the turn of the century. Assuming his status was more or less permanent and a couple of weeks off the payroll didn't knock him out of room and board as well, he had little enough demand on his earnings that the interruption in income wasn't likely to throw him into a serious financial panic.

Motor vehicles, with their parasitic effect on the pocketbook, had yet to become widely available. That, in turn, minimized trips to town and the spending they would almost certainly promote. The ranch furnished horseflesh, bed, board, feed and even ropes. Aside from tobacco if he had the habit, and an occasional side bet on an impromptu horse race, the unmarried puncher needed to invest only in a hat, boots, spurs, saddle and clothing.

Jones' recollections of the typical wardrobe show it to have been anything but extravagant, at least the portion taken out with the wagon. It consisted of a change of socks, a couple of red bandannas usually (also "a black silk bandanna in case you got to go to town or pose for photos"), a couple of longsleeve undershirts and "two pair of longhandle drawers with strings to tie them down." Elastic cuffs on longhandles didn't make their appearance in West Texas until about 1910, he noted, and it was another five years or so before BVDs or boxer shorts showed up on the scene. Even when the shorts were available, they didn't begin displacing longhandles until pickups became commonplace. "A fellow just couldn't ride horseback in those things," Jones wrote.[14]

Horseback work was, of course, the essence of the job at the time. Jones said Renderbrook supplied each man a mount of five horses on the trail, one of which was a night horse. At the ranch the mount increased to six head "with spares available if you didn't mind a little bucking." The spares, naturally, were what was left over after all the cowboys had roped out their chosen strings. There might be any number of reasons for passing over a given horse, but excessive rowdiness was the most common one. Jones said the spares were judged unsafe for women and children.

And so, at times, were some of the regular mounts. Jones noted that a cowboy didn't have to be a top bronc rider to hold a job, but he would periodically be called upon to ride a rough one.[15]

That was inevitable when horses were bought by the carload, as they generally were at the Spades. In the early days many came from the Ellwoods' own stables, particularly buggy and draft animals. Others came from the AAAs and PXs in far West Texas and New Mexico. The usual load was sixteen to eighteen head per thirty-six-foot rail car. These were mostly three- to six-year-old horses, supposedly broken, Jones said, but often "only slightly bent." Many went on to become top mounts, "but others were outlaws for sure." That was the chance a ranch took in buying by carload lots. In return, there was a cost saving. A "good pony," Jones recalled, might sell for $50, whereas they ran about $30 to $35 per head by the car.[16]

For the Spades, those savings could add up. Inventories show Renderbrook kept nearly eighty saddle horses in 1909, the Plains ranch an additional fifty-six head and the 49 Pasture another five. Work horses and mules added fourteen head each to the total at Renderbrook and the Plains ranch, plus two on the 49. There were also five mares and two colts carried on the Renderbrook ledger, a number that grew in later years to as many as twenty-five head.[17]

One of the first things the cowboys did with a new horse was give it a name, Jones said. Sometimes the names were descriptive, sometimes whimsical. Brood mares in the heyday of Hollywood's influence were often named for actresses. Jones remembered Ginger Rogers—"the rangy type but well built"—and Sonja Henie—"more on the Quarter type." Some saddle horses were named for Texas governors including Jim Ferguson, Dan Moody and Jimmy Allred. Irony also crept in: a wiry little coal-black was dubbed "Snowball."[18]

Certain horses had their specialties; a top-flight night horse could literally save a cowboy's life in a stampede, and good roping and cutting horses made those jobs go smoothly. Jones had such a cutting horse he called "Blue Dog," but the pony had a lifelong itch to pitch, and that limited his effectiveness. He had to be "topped off" in a corral before each use, which meant he couldn't be used "outside"—on an open roundup ground in the larger pastures—where his services would be most valued and also where Renderbrook did much of that kind of work.[19]

Renderbrook policy, Jones recalled, allowed a cowboy to pasture two personal mounts—one to ride and one to pack. That, of course, was a rule created in the days when cowboys rode on and off the ranch horseback, before cars and pickups became the common mode of transportation. A man had to have a way to get to the job and a way to leave if he or the boss decided that was the proper course of action. The two-head limit, meanwhile, kept a hand from building up a private horse herd at the expense of Renderbrook grass. Once he got there, a cowboy seldom used his personal mounts. "You turned them out in the Big Pasture and saved them until you got fired or quit."[20]

Like most of the other big outfits, Renderbrook had an annual routine that had been established early and varied little over the years and decades until something happened to force a change or some new development allowed an improvement.

Spring work generally began about the tenth of April, Jones remembered. The cook would start "a couple of days early" to set up the first camp. Four mules pulled the chuckwagon with its ten-foot bed and narrow "hashknife" wheels, loaded high with supplies and the crew's bedrolls.

A trail camp or one of the fall camps when the men were building a herd to be moved would entail a night guard, and these camps were almost always marked by a coal-oil lantern. It would be placed atop the chuck box—usually tied down to keep it from blowing off in the wind and setting the country afire—so the night herders could find the wagon when their shift was up. There was seldom any herd to hold in the spring, thus no night guard and no need for the light. Unless a drouth was on and cattle needed to be moved, or some other circumstance necessitated it, cattle gathered in the spring were dealt with the same day and turned loose before nightfall.

Jones said it was common to round up "about ten to fifteen sections" in the morning and brand and mark the calves from that gather in the afternoon. Depending upon the catch, it might be a long or a short afternoon's work. Sometimes there might be enough daylight left to repeat the process, but that generally wasn't done. "Cows and calves separate in the afternoon," he explained, "so we would only do one roundup a day."[21]

There were several reasons to keep pairs intact. One of the foremost was to avoid separating them so badly that some calves were dogied—prematurely weaned and left stunted or even starved to death as a result. Such a round-up might also net a lot more cows than calves, because it was instinct (particularly among younger calves) to lie up determinedly where their mothers left them when they wandered off to graze; these could be easy to overlook and devilishly difficult to flush.

Then there was the matter of a calf's identity. This became somewhat less of an issue as time went by and confidence in fencing grew, but open range practices and customs died slowly. For years it was a matter of honor to be certain of the brand on a cow before touching a hot iron to her calf; she and her offspring might belong to a neighbor. Long after fences laced the land, it was common to send a "rep" on a neighboring outfit's roundup to look after your interests, and to treat his man in turn with the courtesy you expected for your own. Jones himself often served as "outside" man for Renderbrook in his early years of employment before increasing responsibilities kept him home.

The need to pair cows and calves for identity was reportedly a major factor in the slow acceptance of the Angus breed versus Herefords. Performance of the two was similar and the blacks boasted virtual immunity to pinkeye, long a drawback of Herefords because of their sun-sensitive white faces with a lack of protective pigment in the delicate skin around the eyes. An additional advantage enjoyed by the Angus when it came to shipping time was their naturally polled condition—no horns to remove—but this was ironically said to be their greatest liability as mother cows in the early days. Not only did their lack of horns render them nearly defenseless against wolves and coyotes (this may explain their longstanding reputation as fierce and accurate kickers), it also made them too sociable in a herd; without horns to get in the way, went the explanation, Angus cows

Dogies in the Renderbrook corral, 1917 (Southwest Collection, Texas Tech University).

tended to bunch so tightly that it was next to impossible to tell which calf belonged to what cow.

As at most other times, the day's work on the roundup began before daylight. For the cook, it was even earlier; he started in the wee hours to have the fire up and coffee and breakfast ready by the time the other men rolled out. Typical fare in the early days, Jones reported, was French-fried potatoes and chicken-fried steak. That was eventually replaced with bacon and scrambled eggs. Always there were biscuits—sourdough for years, switching to "milk bread" made with clabber sometime after World War II. By then, Otto explained, "the wagon wasn't out long enough" at a stretch "to get sourdough going good."[22] By the time breakfast was over, the horse wrangler would have the remuda up and the men would start roping out the day's mounts from an impromptu corral made of ropes and cowboys. It was anything but a secure enclosure, and it called for a roper who threw gentle, quiet loops. The fewer he needed to throw to get the job done, the better. Often this task would settle on one or two men who were particularly adept at catching horses without stirring up a fuss. A cowboy would name his mount for the morning, then step up with bridle or hackamore as he was led out.

Running loose in the winter months, many horses would tend to forget the more mannerly aspects of domestication, so the first few saddlings in the spring were apt to be a reeducation process. A few horses, of course, woke up to a new world every morning, and their education was a continuous thing. Because of this, mounting up in the morning usually waited until all the horses were caught and the remaining remuda eased back out to graze. There was no sense taking a chance on scattering the whole bunch and getting someone run over while topping out a few silly broncs.

With everything settled back down, the crew would line out toward the area chosen for that morning's roundup. Taking a lesson from open-range days, it was common practice in the larger pastures to let the terrain define such an area as much as possible. Cows naturally chose their own range, given enough space and sufficient water and grazing. Year in and year out, many of the same cows could be found in the same places, bounded by creeks, ridges, brush thickets or the like. By working such areas in their entirety, a crew could be fairly confident of getting most of the animals within them, almost as if they were fenced separately. Overlapping a little the next day, they could pick up many of the unworked cattle that might have drifted into an area worked the day before. Some of Renderbrook's largest pastures lay astraddle the Colorado, and the river often served to divide one day's range from the next.[23]

1926: the last roundup on the North Spade before it was broken up into farms (Spade Ranches Collection).

Jones described the typical roundup crew as "about eight men" plus the boss, horse wrangler and cook. Depending upon the need, it could swell by "maybe a couple more" men, especially if a herd was to be built, held and driven.[24] This crew would work its way quietly to the back of the day's target area, space out and turn back toward the branding ground, driving everything before it. If a fence or other suitable boundary were handy on one side or the other, cattle might be thrown toward it, otherwise they were kept pushed toward the center of the drive. The pace was as slow as practical, giving young calves time to keep up. On open ground the drive would usually proceed smoothly, a herd gradually building before the riders as cows and their calves were picked up by ones, twos or small bunches. Where it encountered brushy draws or other cover, the line might break down temporarily as cowboys worked their way through the obstructions, raising a vocal ruckus to help flush wily cattle bent on hiding out.

Once the herd gained size and momentum, it would do much of the flushing itself, the bawling drawing more sociable cows like a magnet and the moving mass pushing those of an opposite nature ahead of its advance. Eventually the crew would have its morning's accumulation bunched on the branding grounds or, less often, in pens. Jones counted three "real corrals" on Renderbrook through his years, "big ones that would hold a thousand head," as well as several "minor sets of pens." These were generally situated to serve as many pastures as possible, but they by no means served the entire ranch.[25]

Much of the branding thus occurred on open ground. If available, a fence—or better, a corner—might serve as a backstop for the herd. This was particularly handy when dry cows or some other category were to be cut out and held separate from the main herd. In that case there would be two bunches needing herding, with the added difficulty of keeping them apart against their natural inclination to gather.

The branding and marking itself was essentially the same whether done outside or in one of the corrals. Standard procedure was to rope calves out of the herd from horseback and drag them to the fire. There two-man crews working afoot would release the rope and hold the calves for branding, earmarking and castrating. If the holders were quick and sure, the calves would still be down and there would be no need to leg, flank or otherwise wrestle them to the ground. The big Spade brand went on the left side, so the holders would roll a calf left side up, the front man would pin the neck with a shin and hold the upper foreleg back, and the rear man would pin the lower hind leg forward above the hock with the shank of his boot while pulling back on the upper leg. Held like that the calf was help-less to resist. Circulating among the holders and their "patients" would be the knife man and the brander. The latter would shuttle back and forth from the fire, replacing a cool iron in the coals to reheat and selecting a hot one for the next calf.

Open wounds left by the rough surgical process that ac-companied branding offered screwworm flies an ideal place to lay eggs that would hatch into flesh-eating maggots, so most ranches eventually adopted a foul-smelling tar-like dope known as "tecole" to smear on the fresh, bleeding cuts. This helped deter fly strikes but wasn't foolproof and it did nothing to prevent infestation through peeling brands. By the early 1930s Renderbrook moved its branding season to the fall when cool weather could usually be counted on to slow fly activity.[26] If nothing else, the coming winter would dead-end what generation of flies the brand-ing wounds might harbor.

Screwworms had been a scourge to stockmen in the deep South and more southerly reaches of Texas for years before they became a serious threat to outfits farther north. Jones recalled 1914 as the first really bad screwworm year on Renderbrook. He believed they entered the immediate area with a herd brought from Coleman County. Afterward they were endemic. That particular year was also a wet one, which always intensified insect problems.[27] Another espe-cially bad year, he remembered, was 1919. It too was wet, coming on the heels of the era's big drouth.

Spring work on Renderbrook usually lasted about thirty days by Jones' count, then the summer routine took over. After 1914, it was pretty well consumed "riding for worms."

That was a dirty, smelly business, not suited for the man with a weak stomach. Singly or more often in pairs, riders would scour the countryside for cattle with maggot-infested wounds. These might be branding or marking wounds, umbilical cords on young calves, or cuts made by wire or thorns. Any opening was an invitation to a screwworm fly, who would deposit her eggs therein. Unlike most fly species, the screwworm maggot feeds on living flesh, enlarging the original wound relentlessly and providing ever-increasing habitat for more of its kind. Untreated, a small fly-blown wound would continue to grow until the poor tormented host died of shock, loss of blood or the invasion of a vital organ.

It was the cowboy's job to see that this happened to as few head of stock as possible. He did that by roping and throwing an infested animal, cleaning the stinking wound as well as he could, then treating it with whatever medical aid was available at the time. The earliest was cresylic ointment, but it was only marginally effective. Cotton soaked in chloroform came later; it killed the maggots well enough but required a separate repellent smear to prevent fresh blows. An early smear was made essentially of pine tar. Better than nothing but not a whole lot, it was known to burn the hair off an animal. Bone oil replaced the pine-tar smear and dominated the scene until the development of Formula 62 in the late 1930s.[28]

Though it would be the 1980s before a screwworm eradication program would prove effective, research took a new turn even before World War II when scientists focused on the monogamous nature of the female screwworm fly. The solution would be to sterilize massive numbers of male flies and render the single mating of the females unproductive. Radiation sterilization studies that grew out of the tragedies of Hiroshima and Nagasaki provided the key, and a workable eradication program was tested on the island of Curacao off Venezuela. When the program subsequently proved successful in Florida it moved to the Southwest with strong backing from stockmen.[29]

By the early 1960s ranchers throughout the Southwest became familiar with the drone of DC-3 airplanes and the litter of little flattish boxes they disgorged by the hundreds. In these boxes, marked on the outside with concentric rings like a rifle target, were swarms of sterile screwworm flies. The boxes would tear open in the air, scattering their contents over vast areas of ranchland. Drops were concentrated on areas where screwworm infestations were heaviest.

For years, however, the screwworm "dope kit" was the mark of a working cowboy's saddle. Often constructed of an old boot top with a wooden bottom tacked in, it was more or less permanently tied to the rear saddle strings and seldom removed except for patching or replacement. Around many a country roping, its presence or absence was a reliable indicator of whether the saddle's owner got most of his roping practice in the arena or the pasture.

Depending upon the need, fall work on Renderbrook might start well before summer ended, as it did the dry year when Otto Jones first met the crew dipping cows to move toward better grass elsewhere. Its focus was shipping, first on the trail, later by rail, and still later in trucks. In Renderbrook's trailing days, particularly before the fever tick problem had been conquered, shipping was a slow process that naturally required a timely start if it was to be completed before the dead of winter. When a cow herd had to be built, dipped, and trailed as well, start-up came even earlier.

Jones remembered that first fall at Renderbrook; he signed on with the wagon in August, was soon on the trail with the cow herd to the 49 Pasture, and started in on the regular fall work when he returned. That involved gathering steer yearlings, dipping them twice, driving them to the 49, and repeating the process with two year-old steers destined for the Plains ranch. "It was nearly Christmas before I first saw headquarters," Jones recalled in later years.[30]

A steer drive for Renderbrook generally involved 1200–1500 head, handled by an eight-man crew plus the trailboss, horse jingler and cook.[31] These weren't the months-long drives of open range days, of course, but the principles and most of the techniques remained the same.

Despite the somewhat gentler nature of Durham and later Hereford cattle as opposed to the native types that trekked the old trails to Kansas, Renderbrook and other latter-day trailing outfits still posted night guard. There were usually three shifts, beginning early because trail-tired cattle tended to bed down promptly when given the option. That made the first guard relatively easy. It wasn't necessarily the favorite assignment among the cowboys, however, despite the fact that it gave them the next two shifts for uninterrupted sleep. By the time the first guard began, the men were about as tired as the cattle, their systems subject in addition to the lulling effects of a heavy supper.

Jones recalled that many men preferred the middle shift. It was potentially busier because cattle had a penchant for getting up and stirring about that time of night; if a wreck was going to happen, middle guard usually caught it. Nevertheless, standing middle guard gave the cowboy a chance to sleep off his evening meal and the weariness of the day, then a second spell to grab some more rest before the next day began. A conscientious wagonboss was likely to get his own rest in fractured pieces, checking in for a while with each shift. If weather threatened, he might be up all night and make little or no contact with his bedroll. Such were the rewards of responsibility.[32]

By Jones' day the country was pretty well fenced up, though most of the outfits between Renderbrook and the more northerly Spade divisions were large and in the early years their fences might be miles apart. That helped keep fence crossings to a minimum, and it was fortunate, because they often were, literally, "crossings." It would be a while before gates appeared many places other than traveled roads, so the usual practice was to pull the staples from several posts and let the wires down. Areas of frequent passages had "drop gaps" specially constructed to facilitate crossings. A passion for tight fences developed later which made such practices difficult or downright impossible because there wasn't enough slack in the wires. By then, however, trailing had about drawn to a close and gates were up in most locations where passage remained necessary. Renderbrook itself used red wooden gates at frequent intervals, visible for a long distance in open country. Jones remembered many older cows that never quite caught on to the gates, though, no matter how obvious they were. They had learned as calves to look for a downed section of fence and would walk right by an open gate still looking.[33]

Trailing ended for Renderbrook shortly after Jones became manager, though it resumed for a spell a few years later during a period of tight money. Most ranches in the vicinity had abandoned it as general practice years before, shipping cattle to market on the Texas & Pacific which passed through Colorado City by 1881 and was well established by the time the Ellwoods made their first visit. Other than the walking necessary to get to various rail-side pens, area cattle generally rode to the big stockyards in Fort Worth or farther north long before the turn of the century.

That didn't work for the Spades, however, because the rails didn't go anywhere near the Plains ranch, nor near enough to the 49 Pasture to make shipping practical. As long as Renderbrook steers continued to get their growth on these divisions, they would have to get there afoot. At least until the railroads arrived.

Colonization and the Turning of a Page

T HE RAILROAD finally built nearer the Spades about 1913, when the Santa Fe completed a line from Sweetwater to Lubbock. The 49 Pasture was gone by then, and future Renderbrook calf crops would travel to the Spade in leisure like those from surrounding ranches. The wagon would stay home on the Colorado.[1]

One of the last drives before the rails came was a 1913 trek to a point within present-day Lubbock. Strictly speaking, it wasn't a Renderbrook drive; at least it didn't involve Renderbrook cattle. It did, however, use Otto Jones and a Renderbrook crew. Neighbor Charlie Ware was selling out at the time, and W. L. Ellwood bought the cattle under his TUF brand. Included were 800 head of two- and three-year-old heifers that Ellwood and Dick Arnett purchased in partnership and resold to E. Y. Lee for delivery a few miles outside the young township of Lubbock.

Jones' route for that drive apparently followed his normal path most of the way, diverging only toward the end where it normally would have gone several miles farther west. Jones watered the herd at a playa lake that is now an address on Lubbock's South University. He remarked several years ago that the lake site still caught water, though the residents of the apartment building which by then had come to occupy the spot probably didn't appreciate that as much as Jones had when his thirsty herd hit there in 1913.

While the heifers were watering, Jones took the opportunity to ride over and get a look at the town. There wasn't much to see yet. "There was just a little square around the courthouse," he recalled. The buildings sported wooden sidewalks raised so high off the ground that a man could sit and dangle his feet. Despite its modest size, Lubbock was up with the times. "I counted thirteen automobiles" around the square, he said, all with wooden-spoked wheels. "They scared my pony. I had to hold him."

From the lake Jones' route ran north between today's downtown and the campus of Texas Tech. It was way wide of the community in those days. He delivered the herd at a canyon just north of the present Tech campus.

That was the end of trailing for several years. Then, in the early 1920s, Renderbrook briefly resumed the old practice.[2] It was shortly after the end of the 1916–1918 drouth. When such a hard dry spell breaks, it almost always does so dramatically. Nature seems to go out of her way to make up for stinginess; rain falls in abundance for a time and the country responds as if it had banked its growth potential and was suddenly determined to spend the savings with abandon. The largess never lasts long, of course, and ranchers who restock to match the level of the temporary bounty rather than their pre-drouth norm inevitably find the land overtaxed again in short order. This happened to Renderbrook by about 1920, and once again it became necessary to move some cattle north to relieve the pressure.

Meanwhile, money had become tight, probably in part because sales for several years had been made at drouth-depressed prices and purchases that followed during re-stocking had to be made at rain-swollen highs. Whatever the reasons, Renderbrook was cutting back on expenses wherever possible. W. L. Ellwood asked Jones if he thought it might be possible to return to the trail for a while to save the railroads' high shipping costs. With the extra volume of movement anticipated, the savings—or costs, depending on which way they went—could be greater than normal and have a significant effect on the outfit's overall finances.

The idea suited Jones just fine. He didn't come right out and say he'd missed driving a herd the past few years, but he did tell Ellwood with a hint of mischievous anticipation that he had some young hands who had never known the "pleasure" of standing night guard. Renderbrook herds thus went up the trail again from about 1921 to 1923.

Jones found that things had changed somewhat in the interim. Fencing and farming had gradually increased throughout the period when cattle trailing was common, but annual alterations in the route kept the changes minor from one year to the next. Skipping a few years left a number of developments to be compensated for at once. Jones was forced to thread his herd through a course that led by Iatan, west of Colorado City, then through Indian Canyon near O'Donnell east of Lamesa and finally to Tahoka. He broke out into the T Bar pasture there and traveled pretty freely the remainder of the way to the south end of the Spade, keeping west of the highway that led to Lubbock.

Some of the route changes had to do directly with fencing and other new physical obstacles, some with an increasingly negative outlook toward big herds by landowners along the way. People had begun to object to hosting large numbers of other outfits' cattle on their range, worrying about grazing their own cattle might be losing. Older generations of cowmen who had made trail drives themselves were dying out, and the younger ones lacked an appreciation for the practice. Several of Jones' men were new to that aspect of the cowboying profession too, as he had remarked to Ellwood. It made for some sticky situations on occasion when inexperience conspired with bad luck to turn a minor incident into a regular wreck.

That sort of thing happened early in the new cycle of drives when Jones "overjumped" himself by throwing a 1900-head steer herd on the trail instead of the 1200 to 1500 head he had usually handled. He took only one extra man in addition to the normal eight-man crew. He had his hands full all the way, and one night at Rattlesnake Tank in the Slaughter Pasture the situation got out of hand entirely. When on the trail, he made a habit of bedding the herd in a corner or other fence jog wherever possible so his night guards would have only one or two sides to patrol. That particular night found them hemmed in a section jog when a rainstorm blew up. The remuda was nearby and, as horses are prone to do, many began running, pitching and playing in the rain. The problem was that some of the worst cut-ups wore bells to help the jingler locate the remuda in the pre-dawn darkness. The noise startled the steers and they stampeded. With the barbed wire fence out there in the dark the crew couldn't afford to go riding pell-mell around the herd to circle it; they could only try to hold the open side of the jog and hope the wreck would work itself out. Eventually it did, but when the sun came up the cowboys found a world of fence torn up and cattle scattered on both sides of what was left of it.[3] Jones went back to smaller, more manageable herds for the duration.

Around 1910 a new chore was added to the annual cycle of jobs. "Along about the first of February we'd commence to picking up the thin cattle" out of the large pastures and taking them to smaller pastures for feed, Jones recalled years later.[4] Prompted by the periodic die-ups that had occurred ever since the first big one in 1880, supplemental feeding was a fairly new practice on West Texas ranches when Renderbrook adopted it. That the practice was so long in coming can't be laid at the feet of recalcitrant or tight-fisted ranchers trying to save a buck; most of them saw the need long before they had the means. They generally began feeding as soon as it became practical and reasonably affordable.

That day, however, had to wait for farmers and for processing methods that would turn bulky raw cottonseed into a more concentrated product that could be transported with the equipment then available over still-primitive roads. For years it made more sense to ship the cattle to the feed than the other way around, and a lot of cows that in later years would have stayed for another calf crop or two used to go to market before winter if they showed even fairly minor signs of infirmity. Old Renderbrook records transcribed and saved by Jones indicate that the ranch moved nearly 7000 head of cattle of various ages to feed, graze and market in the fall of 1910. Undoubtedly, many of these were beef steers including an unspecified number that went to Ellwood feed pens in DeKalb. Jones' notes, however, suggest that a sizeable number of cows and calves and even some bulls were shipped to Gainesville, Texas, and Roff, Oklahoma, for winter feeding. Other unidentified cattle went "to Ft. Worth mkt."[5]

Jones' notes show that Renderbrook "fed first cracked cottonseed cake" that winter, a supply of 250 sacks bought from a Colorado City oil mill for $20 per ton, or a total of $350. Two years later the price had climbed to $25 per ton, and by 1913 Renderbrook was also buying alfalfa hay.

Jones' records show the ranch bought 400 bales at fifty cents per bale from James Daly of Sterling City, who grew the hay on fields irrigated from the North Concho River.

Compared with the number of cattle in Renderbrook's inventories, those quantities of feed appear small by modern standards. At the time, however, it was common practice to feed only the cows that needed it most. As Jones noted, particularly thin cows were sorted from the main herd and fed in smaller pastures. It would be several more years before the ranch routinely dispensed winter feed in the large pastures. Even after processed feed became available locally and good quality hay could be had reasonably nearby, there was still the matter of getting it to the ranch. Until 1916 supplies of all sorts, including feed, were still hauled to Renderbrook by freight wagon. It was a slow and expensive process that naturally limited the use of bought goods.

That year, however, the ranch entered the machine age with a heavy truck manufactured by the DeKalb Wagon Company. The only surviving description comes from Jones' notes, which indicate that it had puncture-proof tires of solid rubber, not uncommon for heavy-duty vehicles of the period.[6] Ellwood had had it shipped by rail from his hometown. The truck's first driver was Walter "Coosey" Jackson, who had piloted a freight wagon when not presiding over a Renderbrook campfire.[7] Graduation from freight wagon to freight truck was a common development in the days of transition from muscle to motor power. It was as if the experience of handling balky mules and hairy-legged draft horses was a prerequisite to dealing with ornery, temperamental internal combustion engines that sometimes refused to combust.

When Jackson joined the Navy in World War I, his place at the wheel was taken by H. H. Bennett. It was apparently part of the truck driver's job to care for the mechanical demands of his vehicle much as the wagon freighter saw to the needs of his teams; Bennett became so familiar with the heavy viscosity oil used in the machine's differential that he began comparing it to the molasses used for sweetening on the ranch. Both were bought in drums and both apparently came from the Houston area, so Bennett dubbed the molasses "600-weight." Unlike the oil, however, the syrup was stored in the milk house down at the spring.[8]

Jones also bought his first car about that time. It would be "several years" before Renderbrook furnished him a vehicle, but he used the car to make rounds on the ranch in addition to what little personal travel he did, so Ellwood split the cost of gas and oil with him. By the 1920s cars and pickups became plentiful enough on the ranch to justify a gas pump. Until then Jones would "run to town once a week and fill up."[9]

Neither the truck nor Otto's car were the first motor vehicles to be used regularly on the Spade operations, however. As late as 1912 Uncle Dick Arnett was still horsebound enough to prefer a buggy and team as a retirement gift, but W. L. Ellwood had long been tooling around in a chain-driven Cadillac. Judge Hopping provides the earliest mention of such a vehicle, vaguely dating the event "in the early automobile age."[10] He offers no specifics as to the time, but he drops some clues. One is that the Lubbock garage from which he rented the machine wanted to furnish a driver, an offer which W. L. declined.

The practice of providing a driver—actually a driver/mechanic in most cases—with rented cars dated from the first days of automobile use. Those pioneering vehicles were notoriously finicky about fuel, lubrication and countless mechanical adjustments which were forever coming unadjusted and it took a fairly skilled mechanic to keep one running. The earliest cars were delivered even to their new owners complete with driver/mechanic, whose task it was to teach the fledgling motorist everything from steering and braking to tire repair and partial engine dismantling and reassembly. That practice faded as the concept of local dealerships, or agencies, developed to provide nearby service, and as proliferation of automobiles raised motoring from a rare art to something approaching a pastime. It lingered a bit longer, however, in the rental field; if a neophyte driver destroyed his own car it was, after all, his loss, but ham-handed treatment of a rented vehicle could put a dent in the vendor's pocketbook.

Hopping's other major clue is his description of the Cadillac as chain-driven. That narrows the time frame, assuming the Lubbock garage was anywhere near current in its inventory. Cadillac's chain-driven cars were all single-cylinder models that came on the market in 1902 and went out of production after 1908. As early as 1906 the firm began offering four-cylinder machines, but these were shaft-driven from the beginning.[11] If Hopping is right about the chain drive, W. L. Ellwood was probably motoring across the Plains ranch by 1910, possibly well before.

One account of a motor trip, related to Hopping by Jessie "Jean" Ellwood Chappell, illustrates the irrepressible spirit attributed to Ellwood by those who knew him and the zest for life that he passed on to his daughters.[12] On an outing "to show his family the extent of the Spade ranch and the improvements he had made there," Ellwood had to contend first with a flat and then with a balky engine. This master of far-flung enterprise dismounted, patched, remounted and pumped up his own punctured tire, then proceeded to the nearest windmill to check cattle and his radiator, which in those days was not pressure-capped and tended to boil over at regular intervals. When he stopped at the mill his rented car died and "failed to respond to the crank." A cowboy appeared in short order and hitched on to the car to give it a pull with four-legged horsepower. Consistent with the day's events, however, the horse managed to straddle the rope and went into a pitching fit which ditched the rider and broke the rope. The pony was last seen disappearing over the horizon. That left the whole bunch stranded, but the cowboy, "being the Hercules type," had better luck with the car's crank than had Ellwood. The ranch owner was soon off again with a promise to send someone back with a fresh horse for the dismounted hand. In due time the Ellwoods came to a gate. Reluctant to stop the car for fear it would stall again, W. L. devised a simple but doubtless comical-looking solution: daughter Jean would perch on the running board and jump off as he circled wide by the gate. Ellwood would continue to circle while she opened the gate, then he would drive through and circle again until she could close it and jump back on. In that fashion they continued their tour of the ranch, at every gate leaving strange tracks on either side that surely baffled any passer-by not in on the story.

Hopping makes several other references to W. L.'s early Cadillac. He describes it as a cloth-topped rig with side curtains and "bows like the old wagon bows" to support the top. Ellwood claimed the car only went twenty miles per hour—no more and no less. "It made no difference how rough the road, how many rocks, wagon ruts or dog holes, that was the speed his car made."[13]

Sometimes it wasn't the right speed for the circumstances. Late in 1912 Ellwood, George Arnett and George C. Wolfforth, partnering in cattle at the time, struck out for J. P. White's LFD Ranch in New Mexico to look at a herd of two-year-old steers. The trip out was relatively uneventful and among them the trio bought not only the steers but about 900 head of spayed heifers. On the return leg of their trip they ran up on a cattleguard under construction; only the pit had been completed, and it straddled the road from gatepost to gatepost.

Twenty miles an hour can be a maddeningly slow speed in a modern vehicle with shock absorbers and hydraulic brakes, but Ellwood's Cadillac had neither. And the mechanical brakes of that era were about as effective as dragging a foot. Twenty miles an hour under such primitive conditions, however, was fast enough to slam the car into the ditch violently. It stopped when the front end fetched up against the far side of the pit, nose down. Wolfforth came to rest on the hood after flying through the cloth roof. None of the three cow traders was seriously injured, however. The worst damage was to the car's front suspension, which was nearly separated from the frame. Somehow they extricated the vehicle from the hole and fired it up again. The engine still ran, so off they waddled to the nearby town of Knowls, tracking this way and that as the independent-minded front axle shimmied and swayed. For a while, at least, the Cadillac had a new speed—about five miles an hour counting the zigs and zags.[14]

Once they reached town it took only a short time to get the rig running true again. Hopping doesn't say so, but the repairs were likely handled by a blacksmith. Smithies did a fair amount of business straightening car axles and frames in those days when two-rut roads were the rule.

W. L. Ellwood put in more than his share of miles on such roads, covering the width and breadth of West Texas, buying cattle for his own account, for various partnerships, and for the Spades. From the earliest days, Renderbrook alone couldn't supply enough steers to graze the ocean of Spade grass as the Ellwoods and their managers wanted it grazed. The products of a great number of cow-calf outfits

W. L. Ellwood—rancher with a zest for life—relaxes (Spade Ranches Collection). *"If you've got time to sit down,"* he wrote *"you've got time to lie down."*

walked or rode the rails to the Panhandle ranch over the years, and Ellwood made a broad circuit inspecting and receiving those herds. One of his closest companions for the first several thousand miles was George Arnett, but that partnership came to an untimely end on March 3, 1917, in Canyon. Arnett and two friends were homeward bound from Amarillo when their car skidded off the road on a curve and rolled, killing Arnett but sparing his passengers.[15]

Ellwood's partnerships with Sam Arnett and George Wolfforth continued, and about that time he took on another trading companion, Len "Mack" McClellan. W. L. provided the McClellans with a succession of homes in Lubbock, including the "red house," so named because the house and all its furnishings were red, right down to the china. The McClellans, in turn, provided W. L. a family life of sorts to compensate for his long periods of separation from his own family in Illinois. Mrs. Ellwood visited as often and for as long as practical, but her heart and home remained in DeKalb. W. L.'s were just as firmly anchored in West Texas.[16]

But it was a changing West Texas, and as the teens drew to a close it was set for even greater changes—especially W. L. Ellwood's part of it.

Those changes stemmed in great part from the growing network of steel rails threading their way across what only a few decades before had been the mysterious and forbidding refuge of the Comanche. Once men discovered that water lay in abundance just a relatively few feet beneath the dry plains soil, only a lack of transportation stood in the way of the farmer and his plow. With the rails came those farmers and plows, and the cowman's day was suddenly gone like that of the Indian the white man had displaced. Panhandle soil was too deep, too good and too rich to remain in cow grass, just as it had been too productive a grassland to be left to a few scattered bands of nomadic hunters and the buffalo that sustained them. Colonel Isaac Ellwood had seen that in 1890 when he predicted that his two- and three-dollar rangeland would someday sell as $40 or $50 farmland. W. L. knew it, too, but by all accounts the prospect was as disturbing to him as it had been encouraging to his father. The elder Ellwood had spent his formative years in a place and time when the highest expression of independence and pioneering had been to rip out virgin sod scores of centuries in the making and convert it into grainfields, neat little farms and settled communities. He had realized that dream himself in DeKalb and had cherished the accomplishment even more deeply than his far grander and more remunerative dealings in industry and high finance. Colonel Ellwood loved his vast Texas holdings with their seas of grass stretching to seemingly boundless horizons, but when he looked at them, much of what he saw was their potential as something entirely different.

His son's dreams, by contrast, were forged in West Texas in an adopted culture whose highest expression was manifested in huge herds of grazing cattle tended by skilled men on horseback. W. L. Ellwood had "made a hand," or enough of one to elicit the approval of the demanding Uncle Dick Arnett, and that invisible badge of honor deeply colored his outlook on the family's ranch properties. He might wholeheartedly support more windmills and tanks, more working facilities and better camps, but aside from improvements such as these, the land simply couldn't get any better than it was. Changes of a different sort would not be improvements to his way of thinking. They would be just the opposite.

It must have seemed a powerful irony to him then, as he watched himself deliberately and knowingly take crucial steps to help bring those very changes along.[17] The first rail line to approach the Ellwoods' Plains ranch was the Pecos and Northern Texas, which built from Canyon to Plainview in 1907. By 1911 it had pushed through Lubbock and made connection with the Texas and Pacific at Sweetwater, allowing shipment of Spade cattle between Renderbrook and the Plains. It also facilitated farm fever in the Panhandle area around Lubbock and spawned demand for more lines in the vicinity. W. L. Ellwood had not been involved in that initial railroading incursion and thus could share neither credit nor blame for the changes it brought. It was a different story with the next line, however.

Almost immediately the Santa Fe proposed a route from Lubbock to Farwell, connecting there with its own main line and tying Lubbock to a network reaching Amarillo in the north and El Paso in the south, by way of the developing New Mexico settlements of Roswell and Carlsbad along the Pecos River. The planned line would meet Ellwood's Spade about twenty miles northwest of Lubbock. W. L. had his first opportunity to affect the pace of the area's development—by withholding right-of-way he could perhaps delay if not scotch the plan entirely. At the time he already had access to rails at Bovina, and had been using the pens and siding there to ship Spade cattle to market. It was only a short drive compared to the long treks of earlier years, so the prospect of a loading point on or near Spade property offered little personal inducement to him. At the least, Ellwood might have been expected to extract a handsome price from the railroad in exchange for his cooperation with a program that he knew would only hasten the disintegration of his life's work. Instead, he deeded the necessary right-of-way and more—free. The Lubbock-to-Farwell line was completed in 1914, and the rush to farm the Panhandle quickened.

Piece by piece, in four-section homesteads and smaller plots sold out of state grants to the railroads, land around the Spade went behind fence and under the plow. Larger ranches that had operated mostly on state grazing leases saw their range shrink as parcel after parcel was cut out. Various outfits found their remaining acreage insufficient to support viable herds and were finally forced to put their deeded land on the market as well.[18]

That wasn't an immediate threat to the Spade because its expanse was all safely deeded. There would be no nesters taking up choice locations on Spade range. With the change from grazing land to farmland came people, however, and a swelling demand for schools, roads and other government services. These had to be funded by taxes, and taxes were based on market value of land. Once again, a strength became a weakness. The Spade's ability to withstand the onslaught of immigrants lay in its well-blocked expanse of deeded acreage with no vulnerable cracks or chinks; suddenly this monolithic block of land which formed a sizeable part of two counties was called upon to fund the ballooning expenditures run up on some of the land owned by others in those counties. And it was no longer being taxed as three- and four-dollar rangeland. Property just like it was bringing several times that on the open market as corn and cotton fields, and the Spade was valued and taxed accordingly.

It was an untenable situation, but W. L. Ellwood held out. In the mid-teens a 60,000-acre block bordering the Spade on the west went up for sale by Major George W. Littlefield. His Yellowhouse Ranch was virtually all gone by 1918, and land agents were soon hitting Ellwood up with offers to handle the Spade as they had done the Yellowhouse. He declined, but he watched.

Late in 1923, W. E. Halsell offered 70,000 acres south of

Littlefield's former ranch and also bordering the Spade, and most of it was gone by October of the next year. It brought $25 per acre, not yet $40 or $50 as Colonel Isaac Ellwood had foreseen, but a tremendous figure at which to rate rangeland for taxes.

Halsell's agent was Judge R. C. Hopping. As unsold Halsell acreage dwindled in the summer of 1924, Hopping approached Ellwood seeking more land to "colonize." Land prices were climbing as the boom began to feed upon itself, and Hopping told Ellwood he felt confident the Spade range could be turned for $35 an acre "with good terms." Their first meeting occurred in Lubbock's West Texas Hospital, where Ellwood was bedridden for three weeks following an attack of appendicitis. Serious as such a condition is today, it was infinitely more hazardous in 1924, when there were no antibiotics to deal with likely infections. It was, in fact, often a fatal condition either directly or indirectly, so W. L. may have been contemplating his own mortality when Hopping came to call. Whether or not that was a factor is unknown; perhaps Hopping was simply as good at creating sellers as he was at creating buyers. Or maybe the tax burden had become too onerous. For whatever reason or reasons, Hopping succeeded in convincing the rancher to open some of the Spade land for farm sales.[19]

Hopping and partner Stanley Watson set up shop in a small frame office beside the Santa Fe tracks. Their Ellwood Farms operation was to concentrate on Spade acreage north of the rail line. Ellwood set no specific limit on the amount of land he would sell, but he insisted that sales be blocked as they went, with no random tracts hopscotching out into virgin range and interfering with ranch operations as long as there remained a ranch to operate.

Price was set at $35 per acre, $5 down and the balance payable within fifteen years at six percent interest. The first

Otto Jones and wife at the Renderbrook White House. The machine age is evident (Southwest Collection, Texas Tech University).

four sales were concluded on Saturday, September 27, 1924, and the following Monday saw another dozen tracts change hands. By January 1925 the two agents had sold 222 farms ranging from eighty acres to a section apiece. Hopping recorded that 25,000 acres of sod had been turned under by the summer of 1925.

Anton, "the town with a purpose," was established on the section that held the Ellwood Farms office. It was named for Santa Fe division superintendent J. F. Anton, who had approved the rail crossing that served the site. Anton also purchased a section of land adjoining the town section, and that certainly may have figured in his choice as a namesake for the new town.

By April 1, 1926, sales had taken 35,000 acres out of the North Spade's 80,000. W. L. Ellwood bowed to the inevitable and ordered foreman Tom Arnett to roll out the wagon. The last roundup on the North Spade was completed before the end of the month, netting 5800 head of steers. The remainder of the North Spade and 18,000 acres of the South Spade were gone by January 1, 1927. Another 50,000 acres went on the block within the next couple of years, but then sales began to drop off. Taxes didn't, of course, so to counter the slack market, W. L. Ellwood reached back to a sales technique that had worked for him decades before in the horse business—he commissioned an advertising pamphlet. Specific elements varied over the next five years, but the basic premise remained unchanged: drawn up by sales agent Hopping, the literature would tout the fertility of the soil, the promise of the growing farming communities, and the blessings of the Panhandle climate.

It was not the pamphlets' purpose to provide a detailed environmental lesson, so little things like blue northers and unpredictable rainfall patterns tended to fall between the lines or even off the pages. In at least one issue, Hopping boldly promised readers a healthy life at Ellwood Farms because "germs cannot exist at this altitude." That surprising assertion doubtless grew from the readily apparent fact that higher and drier climates were free from some ailments that plagued lower and wetter regions. Likewise, most of the remaining claims in the pamphlets were either factually accurate or had sprung from factual roots.

Most important, they seemed to work. Hopping said the flyers "carried the land office" through the low commodity prices of the early 1930s when purchasing farmland was a risky prospect. To the extent that they promoted more land sales than might otherwise have been made at that time, the pamphlets ironically may have contributed to growing financial strains pressing the Ellwood Estate. The scores of thousands of acres selling for $35 each made the estate a paper fortune on rangeland that had cost only a fraction of that figure. It was just that, however—a paper fortune. Land was sold for a few dollars down, most of the purchase price still owed by farmers too desperately pressed to pay the taxes, not to mention interest. As for the principal, that was out of the question.

W. L. Ellwood's approach to the problem was much as his father's might have been had the elder Ellwood lived to deal with it. He neatly melded compassion and good business: if the farmers could pay the interest, the principal would wait for better days; if they couldn't manage even the interest, then their best efforts would suffice. It sounded foolishly generous to some, but it was a pragmatic approach from Ellwood's viewpoint. His major reason for selling, after all, had been the crush of taxation, and if he took the land back that expense would once again fall on the estate's shoulders.

By that time the former Spade lands were supporting about 1200 families, if "supporting" is the proper term. The

South Plains Opportunities

PUBLISHED BY

E L L W O O D   F A R M S

LUBBOCK, TEXAS

Lamb, Hockley, Hale and Lubbock Counties, Texas

Vol. IV   October, 1934

ELLWOOD FARMS MAIN OFFICE, LUBBOCK, TEXAS

Ellwood's advertising pamphlet was designed to entice land buyers (Spade Ranches Collection).

Dust Bowl of the thirties had yet to set in and crops on the fresh and fertile soil were good. The Great Depression was well underway, however, and even the best crops were worth little money. Hopping recorded that maize heads brought only $5 a ton and cotton three cents a pound. At those prices, he continued, a farmer might clear a dollar or two per bale of cotton after direct costs, and production ranged from half a bale to a bale an acre. Figuring what he had borrowed on his crop for living expenses, Hopping added, "a young farmer with a family was more often than not one to three dollars in the hole over each bale."

By 1931 Ellwood was forced to employ an even more generous, imaginative—and costly—policy to help "his" farmers survive. He began accepting cotton in lieu of cash as debt payments. It was a favorable arrangement for those farmers who could take advantage of it because Ellwood credited them at a higher rate than they could make on the cash market. Hopping wrote, for example, that Ellwood would give eight cents' credit for nickel cotton, a dime for seven cents' worth.

The arrangement made Ellwood one of the largest cotton sellers in the area. A *Lubbock Morning Avalanche* story from June 11, 1932, reported the sale of 2000 bales of Ellwood-held cotton from the 1931 crop and noted that he still held about 1700 more at the time. Each and every bale was sold at a loss, but at least it maintained a cash flow. Ellwood also bought "bundle feed" from his grain farmers, storing it in silage pits at Spade headquarters, and he provided every farmer who wanted one with a brood sow. Once again, there was no cash cost to the recipient, only a promise, in Hopping's words, "that he was to give back to Mr. Ellwood two pigs—not necessarily from the first litter, but within a reasonable length of time."

The big-time cowman who had agonized over the pros-

pect of turning his beloved range into farms was now working himself into exhaustion and a precarious financial exis-
tence to keep the invading farmers afloat. Edging past his
allotted three-score years and ten, Ellwood began to show
the strain. He fell asleep and rolled his car on one of his
innumerable trips. His injuries were apparently minor, but
the incident finally convinced him to take a relief driver
along in the future.

The New Deal's agriculture assistance programs began to
ease some of Ellwood's personal financial strains by 1933
with emergency loans to hard-pressed farmers. Through
the Federal Land Bank and the Land Bank Commission,
these loans were to be available for sums up to half the
value of the land pledged against them. As usual, however,
there was a catch. The Land Bank used its own appraisals to
set loan limits, and in the topsy-turvy economic climate of
the 1930s those appraisals were coming in much too low to
help potential South Plains borrowers. So Ellwood took on
the government as his father had taken on moonshine wire
makers. Through the Panhandle Agricultural Association,
established in the summer of 1933, he lobbied the Land
Bank Commissioner for higher valuations. The Association
argued that undervaluing Panhandle farmlands effectively
nullified the Farm Mortgage Act.

But Ellwood carried the effort even further. Recognizing
the immediacy of the problem and the fact that challenging
valuations individually or even in bulk might take longer
than some farmers could bear, he reasoned that the key to
accurate appraisals was a knowledgeable appraiser. His
goal was to have his farmers' land valued according to a
ten-year production record, thus smoothing out the Dust
Bowl dips in production and the Depression's miserable
prices. He also wanted to install an appraiser familiar with
the potential of the relatively new Panhandle cropland. Ell-

wood felt his own land agent, R. C. Hopping, met those qualifications, and he went straight to Land Bank president A. C. Williams with his proposal. It took some talking, but eventually Williams agreed and Hopping was named appraiser for ten Texas counties. He had nine assistant appraisers under him, and answered directly to W. J. McAnnally of Houston, chief appraiser for Texas.

Hopping records that he and McAnnally had some disagreements over values during the roughly six months that he served, a few serious enough to bring McAnnally all the way to the Panhandle to see disputed land himself. Hopping apparently prevailed most of the time, however, and he said values in his area were "pretty well established" by the end of 1933. That was fortunate for the Ellwood interests, because they suddenly found themselves in serious need of Hopping's services again themselves. Three days after Christmas in 1933, W. L. Ellwood passed away. He hadn't been able to leave the family's affairs quite as well organized as his father had nearly a quarter century earlier.

The complexities of the massive land sales and the difficulties imposed by the Depression would have complicated matters under the best of circumstances, but this time the passing of the reins was further hampered by a lack of anyone to pass them to. When Colonel Ellwood died, W. L. had already become almost a permanent fixture in Texas. He was there more than he was home, and most of the Texas dealings for several years had been under his guidance and control to begin with. As younger brother Perry stepped into their father's shoes in DeKalb, W. L. simply lengthened his stride in Texas.

At the time of his own passing, however, there was no family member situated to take W. L.'s place. Despite their interest in the Texas operations, his daughters had been raised to love the ranches, not to run them. In addition, both had married and established families in New England; moving to Texas was out of the question. Perry Ellwood's family and responsibilities likewise tied him to DeKalb. He would visit Texas more in the remaining years of his life, but he could not move there.

The job fell to Will Eisenberg of DeKalb.[20] From his hiring by longtime Ellwood secretary A. W. Fisk in 1910, Eisenberg had progressed quickly to the point where his competence and trustworthiness made him the obvious successor when Fisk himself died in 1918. By 1933 Eisenberg knew almost as much about the Ellwood business dealings as those who had conducted them. His status within the overall operation was such that W. L. appointed him co-executor of the Ellwood Estate along with Perry Ellwood.

Dust Bowl Days

8

E ISENBERG worried over the new assignment "for days," Hopping records, "yes months before he could make up his mind that he was equal to the many responsibilities."[1] That must have made his first weeks in Texas especially difficult, because he was immediately thrust into the role of decision-maker with some major decisions to make.

Eisenberg and Perry Ellwood, as W. L. had before them, elected to make no serious changes in their predecessor's programs. Policies and management would continue along the course W. L. had set. Even without any shakeup or reorganization to conduct, however, Eisenberg had no time to settle gradually into his new job. When he arrived in Lubbock he found a series of loans pending on purchases from Ellwood Farms. These had been approved by the Land Bank but had not received concurrence from W. L. The problem facing Eisenberg was that the loans were for considerably less than the borrowers owed the Ellwood Estate. Releasing the land as collateral to the Land Bank meant writing off the interest originally agreed upon and in some cases even giving up a portion of the principal. For someone harboring doubts about his own abilities in the face of such a challenge, it had to be an exceedingly difficult moment. As Hopping wrote, however, "there was not much choice." The estate had little or no money coming in from its sales and taxes on remaining land were mounting. The federal loans were the only game in town at the time, so Eisenberg swallowed hard and approved those that were not unreasonable.

An indirect side effect of accepting reduced terms on the Land Bank loans, particularly those in which the principal was trimmed, was that they might devalue future sales as well, a possibility that doubtless plagued Eisenberg's deliberations.

If indeed he wondered about this, he didn't have long to await the answer. Another government assistance project, Texas Rural Communities, was in the market for 4000 acres of land on which to settle farm families then on the relief rolls. Ellwood Estates offered a bid asking $120,000 for such a plot near Ropesville. That worked out to $5 per acre less than previous Spade land sales, but in March of 1934 the program's officials tendered a counter offer of only $100,000. Devaluation was clearly underway. Eisenberg and Perry Ellwood agreed to the reduction, taking $25 an acre for land that only a few years before had sold easily at $35. The deal was concluded in January, 1935, and the influx of cash temporarily eased the estate's burdens.

At least the transaction eased the crushing pressure of taxes and operating expenses. There was still one heavy burden clouding the picture that would take a whole herd of $100,000 deals to dispel. I. L. Ellwood's will had stipulated that his daughters receive cash for their shares of the estate and that W. L. and Perry retain ownership of the Spade and Renderbrook lands. At the time of W. L. Ellwood's death the balance still owed to his sisters was in the neighborhood of $2 million. With the Spades' cash flow problems, considerable time elapsed without any payments on that debt. Finally the sisters employed an attorney to collect.[2]

The lawyer notified Will Eisenberg in advance of his impending visit. Prior notice wasn't a matter of courtesy, however; the agent informed Eisenberg that he had been instructed to accept only cash. Under no circumstances would he settle for a draft on Citizen's National Bank, because the sisters were well aware of the Ellwood-Arnett influence at the bank. They made no effort, apparently, to conceal their suspicion that such a draft might not be honored once the lawyer was out of the neighborhood. That attitude didn't set well with Perry Ellwood, W. F. Eisenberg, or their friends among the Arnett clan. The amount of the demand is no longer remembered, but it was undoubtedly more than the Spade owners could afford at the time. Nevertheless, they would have found a way to raise it had the demand not been accompanied by such a thinly veiled insult. Eisenberg put his inventive nature and bookkeeper's shrewdness to work on the problem, searching for a way to meet the attorney's terms without actually turning over cash they didn't have.

The solution was worthy of Charles Goodnight, who once had a wheelbarrow load of pennies hauled to the Texas State Land Office to pay for his grazing lease after a similar insult. Eisenberg didn't go quite that far—he settled for small bills. Even so it required a shipment from a Fort Worth bank. There wasn't enough cash of any denomination in Lubbock during those hard times, much less the fives, tens and twenties Eisenberg wanted.

When the sisters' attorney arrived, Eisenberg greeted him cordially, ushered him into his office, and began pull-

Perry Ellwood (Spade Ranches Collection).

ing stacks of money out of his desk drawers. When the top of the desk was covered several inches deep with currency, the lawyer evidently fell prey to the thoughts Eisenberg had hoped would occur to him—that if these folks were bad enough to be suspected of welshing on a bank draft, they might also be capable of hiring someone to knock him in the head and recover the cash once he'd signed for it and left the premises. West Texas, after all, was still considered a rough region by most outlanders. The attorney told Eisenberg to put the money back.

"I'll take your offer as an indication of good faith," he explained somewhat nervously, "and recommend that my clients bide their time."

The episode provided the injured parties enough satisfaction to ease the sting of the insult, and it bought the operation enough time to retire the debt as had always been planned. That took a few more years and the return of a measure of prosperity, but there had never been any intention of ignoring Spade obligations.

Meanwhile, the Renderbrook end of the Spade enterprise was having its own problems. What the Dust Bowl did to farming throughout the Great Plains it also did to ranching, though in its own way. Will Rogers tried to help farmers grin their way through the worst of it, remarking in one early thirties radio broadcast that since archaeologists had found all the world's great civilizations buried under layers of dirt, perhaps the clouds of dust roiling over his home state of Oklahoma and its neighbors signified the region's advancement That would not happen, he felt sure, to Southern California—"at least not for the same reason."

The soil from unturned rangeland by and large didn't blow away, but the grass parched and burned. Cattle went hungry, and there was no place to move them to as Renderbrook cowboys had in previous drouths. The ranch turned from straight cottonseed meal to grain cubes for its winter supplement. The meal had provided mostly protein and served well enough when the pastures had enough old grass to supply energy.[3] Without grass, energy as well as protein had to come from another source, and the combination cubes served that function.

It wasn't cheap, however. Otto Jones recalled many years later that feed costs climbed "up to $60 a ton in the worst years," a price that wouldn't be seen again until the next crippling drouth twenty years later. Raw feedstocks, of course, were just as scarce as range grass at the time, and demand was heavy. In the depths of the long dry spell Renderbrook was forced to extend its winter feeding program into the summer, adding to the financial misery.

Then the water started to go.[4] Renderbrook's attraction first to the Indians and later the soldiers had been its spring and creek water. Taylor Barr undoubtedly chose the area as headquarters for his informal cow outfit with those natural attributes in mind, the Snyders followed him for the same reason, and the Ellwoods concurred. During the 1930s, however, creek and stream flow gradually diminished and finally quit. Jones recalled that Renderbrook Spring "held its own fairly good" until 1934, flowing an estimated fifty gallons per minute year in and year out. That summer it slowed to "barely a fifth" of that rate.

The outfit's response was to dam up creeks and draws in an effort to catch and hold water when it did run. That practice was later prohibited in favor of "pit" tanks on sloping ground, but at the time the government encouraged it with about a fifty-fifty cost share. In one form or another, the ranch dammed or dug upwards of eighty tanks. But these were passive watering structures; they did no good if nature refused to fill them, and the very drouth that made them necessary kept them marginally effective at best.

Renderbrook turned to water wells to take up the slack, but it was a costly undertaking. Jones remembered drilling prices rising from about seventy-five cents a foot to a dollar and finally $1.25. Most of the wells they hit were above the clay formation known as the "red beds" and were less than a hundred feet deep, but most of the holes they tried came up dry. Only about one in five made wells at whatever depth. Renderbrook began laying pipe into dry pastures to stretch the value of the few wells they made. Most of the lines were inch-and-a-half galvanized-steel pipe at seven to eight cents a foot. Individual lines stretched as long as seven or eight miles. To defeat gravity, some stretches were equipped with air cocks, an ingenious device that uses the water's own weight to lift it uphill.

Renderbrook also began modernizing its string of windmills, hoping to make up in efficiency some of what it was being shorted in quantity.[5] Most of the original windmills had been of the old Eclipse style with fans made up of a complex and somewhat fragile web of cypress blades. The blades were prone to loosening, which sometimes allowed the entire fan to become unbalanced. Left unrepaired for too long, it could self-destruct. That such self-destruction didn't happen more often than it did is attributable mostly to another Eclipse shortcoming—the motor had no oil bath and required frequent greasing, so the mills were seldom neglected for long. The old Eclipse motors also lacked reduction gearing, meaning it generally took a stiff breeze to get them pumping. By the early thirties the ranch began taking down the Eclipse mills and replacing them with geared Axtells bought in San Angelo.

Former cowhand Fred McClellan remembered that the man in charge of the swap-out was named Logan. McClellan recalled Logan's helper better, though. The helper's name was Slim Singleton, though the cowboys called him

Slim Axtell. "He was a great big old tall boy, a real windmill man who done most of the work. He was just like a monkey up there."

All these expensive improvements were forced on the ranch at a time when it was next to impossible to recover their costs. With the drouth so widespread, cattle were coming off the country everywhere. And with the nation mired in depression and so many people out of work, few could afford to buy what beef the drouthed-out cattle produced. The dilemma led to yet another government program, one that had a devastating psychological impact on many of the individuals who participated.

To ease the crunch on producers, the federal government stepped in and bought huge numbers of cattle. Some of the best were relocated to more fortunate areas. Renderbrook received about $20 per head for those kind. Lesser sorts went to slaughter, and those that were poorer still were killed right on the ranch. It was a pattern repeated throughout the Southwest and remembered with crystal clarity by most who had a hand in it or watched it happen.

"I hate to tell you what they done with them," Otto Jones told a visitor decades later.[6] He related the story anyway, reluctantly, as a war veteran might relate an episode that he'd much rather not remember but which he considered too important to forget. As Jones described it, the slaughter on Renderbrook was conducted at the Beef Pens near the center of the ranch. It totaled about 3000 head, most of them shot by a government inspector armed with a .22 rifle.

"We had a deal with some of the neighbors," Jones said, to trade the hides for labor to dispose of the carcasses. A small canyon near the pens was dammed and the skinned cattle were rolled off into the mass grave. The carcasses were topped with a huge pile of mesquite brush and the whole thing set ablaze. "The fire burned about a week," he remembered, and the ashes that remained were eventually covered with dirt.

One of the inspectors' jobs was to see that none of the carcasses were diverted, none of the meat salvaged for human consumption. The program, after all, was intended to help stabilize meat prices in the face of a glut. Most inspectors were presumably diligent within reason, but there are times when diligence and human decency part company. Former hands who'd been present for the Renderbrook kill remembered later that the inspector there seemed eager to busy himself with chores that took his attention away from the scene as soon as the shooting stopped. Thus occupied, he managed not to notice as all around him meat was carried off by gaunt townfolk who had assembled there.[7]

The cowboys themselves saw no reason to break his concentration, government work being important and all.

Along with wells, tanks, water lines and a new feeding regime, the 1930s drouth and depression also brought a new kind of fence to the ranch that barbed wire built—and a different class of livestock to run behind it. Renderbrook had been a straight cow outfit from at least the 1880s when the Snyder brothers began firming up title and building fence. Itinerant herders may have grazed sheep across the land after that, but there were no resident sheep within Renderbrook's boundaries. Until 1935.

Otto Jones in several accounts dated the first netwire sheep fences on the ranch at 1929, but in those same accounts maintained that the first sheep to graze behind them didn't arrive until 1935.[8] The mid-thirties date is logical, coming after both dry weather and economic difficulties had set in, and forcing the Spades' management to seek diversification. It would also put the onset of sheep production after W. L. Ellwood's death, suggesting considerable resistance to the idea on his part. Jones attributed the move toward sheep to Perry Ellwood and Pete Ainsworth, stating with certainty that there were no sheep on Renderbrook while W. L. was living.

That the elder brother would allow sheep fencing while apparently opposing the sheep themselves isn't explained, but Jones remembered that something over twenty sections were strung with "Ellwood" net in 1929. The area under sheep fence grew to about seventy sections in the next two decades.[9] Incorporating sheep into the cow outfit also required separate working facilities, scaled down to the smaller animals' size. Otherwise, Jones said, there were few real changes in working methods. Renderbrook never used dogs or herders and except for shearing hired no other help to handle sheep.

"We used our regular cowboys," he told an interviewer many years later, and never lost a hand over refusal to work with the woollies. Not that there wasn't resistance. Jones wasn't fond of the idea at first, "but after we'd had them awhile, I came to like them well enough."[10] Sheep numbers during the period ran as high as 10,000 head, usually about 6000 mother ewes. To handle that volume at shearing required twelve-drop machines "a lot of times."[11]

Some old-time cow operators believed sheep and cattle couldn't be grazed on the same land, and a few went so far as to insist that cattle wouldn't drink from water that sheep had used. Those beliefs led to bloody battles in some parts of the country even as combination ranchers in the Edwards Plateau and Southwest Texas were disproving them in routine daily practice. These men discovered early that sheep and cattle could not only co-exist on the same ground, but that the two species barely competed with one another, cattle preferring the taller grasses and sheep thriving best on short grass and weeds. Jones avowed that sheep had, in fact, been good for Renderbrook's range, "keeping broomweed and things like that down so we had more grass."[12]

They also helped the bottom line on the ranch ledger books. An old joke in mixed-stock country—told only partly in jest—is that a combination rancher runs cattle for prestige and sheep to pay for the cattle. It's told by way of acknowledgement that, year in and year out, sheep tend to be more profitable than cattle. One reason for that is the dual-purpose nature of sheep: their offspring, like those of cattle, can be sold for meat animals or replacements, and the mother flock produces an annual "bonus" crop of wool. At times throughout history the wool clip has actually returned more dollars than the lamb crop. Jones recalled Renderbrook wool ranging from twenty-five cents to as much as a dollar a pound during the thirties and forties, averaging about forty to fifty cents.[13]

Whatever the vagaries of prices at any given time, Renderbrook, like other combination outfits, found that wool, lambs and calves gave them three chances to hit a decent market rather than the single opportunity offered by calves alone. Prices for the three separate commodities seldom followed the same trend at the same time, doubtlessly helping to put a favorable coloration on Jones' opinion of the enterprise once he'd been in it awhile.

For all their tribulations and difficulties, the 1930s are neverthless remembered fondly by some of the former Spade cowboys who lived and worked through them. All eras are transitional in a sense, serving as a bridge between the time just past and the time yet to come, but for West Texas cowboys the thirties stand alone in that regard. Changes both real and potential were piling up faster than ever before, in some cases too fast to be sorted out and recognized for what they were before the next developments washed in and covered them up.

The automobile for example, was no longer a novelty by the late twenties, but its full impact on the ranching business was just beginning to become evident. Today's indispensable pickup was relatively slow to evolve, and even then the broad range of its usefulness had to be established application by application. From a handy vehicle to haul feed or groceries from town to a replacement for the wagon in on-ranch chores was a big move for a device only a few years removed from the status of an untrustworthy novelty. After all, if a wagon broke down, its driver could always ride one of the team.

The pickup's advantage in speed won out, however, and began to change ranch life in ways both subtle and far-reaching. To fix a distant windmill or patch a fence on a ranch the size of Renderbrook could stretch into several days' work using a wagon. A man would routinely throw a bedroll and camp outfit in with his tools and supplies and spend the night wherever darkness caught him. Barring breakdowns, a pickup could have the same man almost anywhere and back in the same day. It allowed him to do more in a given period of time, which in turn meant it took fewer of him and his kind.

That fact didn't manifest itself fully or immediately in the management methods of the time, and neither did many other developments such as improved communications, self-oiling windmills, portable power equipment and livestock trucking. Sometimes the new tools actually complicated life, as was the case with the early telephone system strung to various Renderbrook camps. Soon after the phones were installed, Otto Jones called the camp where his brother Fred was "batching" and was surprised to get an answer. Being home, of course, meant his brother wasn't out tending to whatever needed doing.

"What are you doing home in the middle of the day?" Otto demanded.

"Well, somebody's gotta' stay here to answer this damned phone," Fred retorted with perfect logic.[14]

It was the next decade in many cases, when the manpower demands of World War II and later the broadened horizons of its experiences reduced the ranch labor pool, that some earlier labor-saving improvements really paid off. That helped give the thirties a golden glow in retrospect that they might not otherwise have enjoyed. Cowboys remembered the favorable aspects of the changes and improvements, unsullied by what for many of them were negative developments.

High Times and
Horse Wrecks

A COWBOY from the 1880s, lifted bodily from his own time and dropped like a stone into the 1930s, wouldn't have needed long to get his bearings. Particularly on the larger outfits, he would have found more familiar than unfamiliar elements and could have set in and made a hand with only a short spell of slack-jawed head shaking.

Life for the cowboy was still lived mostly horseback but with a car or pickup to take him to town on Saturday night. Big outfits like Renderbrook still used a chuckwagon, though by then it was often as not the old chuckbox chained and boomered to a truck bed. Married cowboys could either commute by motor vehicle to their wives or stay with the rest of the crew as suited their personal preference or immediate degree of marital bliss. In time modern transportation would displace the chuckwagon entirely in favor of noon meals delivered hot from headquarters and a familiar bed every night. The same easy mobility would rob even the camp system of its original mission, though the better camps lingered on as family homes to accommodate the increasing percentage of cowboys who chose the married route.

The pace of life would quicken soon enough, urged along by other distractions hatched in the same nest of progress. Radio reached most areas and television was coming. That made the 1930s the last real bastion of story-telling and practical jokes as the cowboys' chief entertainment. Long-time cowboy and eventually Renderbrook manager J. E. "Shorty" Northcutt recalled it as a time when "nobody had nothin' and you had to do whatever you could to have fun. I could always find something to laugh about."[1]

"You could when it come out your way," chided Ted Sorrells, who cowboyed for Renderbrook as early as the thirties and as late as the early 1980s. Sorrells was at times the butt of Northcutt's practical jokes, though he dished out his share as well. Most of the jokes—and the stories—revolved around horses. One typical horse story opens with Northcutt preparing to top out the first of a pen of three broncs one morning when Sorrells shows up.

"Let's go down to the house for some coffee," Northcutt invited, offering Sorrells his choice of broncs to make the trip of a hundred yards or so. It's become almost a cliché that a true cowboy never walked when there was something handy to ride, and such clichés generally spring from the truth. Rather than dismount from the skittish broncs once they'd hit the house, Northcutt called his wife, Christine, out onto the porch. When she explained that she didn't have any coffee, Sorrells popped off.

"You can make some, can't you?" he snapped, whereupon Mrs. Northcutt turned on her heel and slammed the door.

That startled the Northcutts' big black dog, which had

been napping on the porch. He lunged straight at the horses before he came fully awake. Suddenly set upon by what looked like an attacking dog, the two green horses elected to emigrate. Northcutt's horse settled down before long, but the one Sorrells had chosen wasn't so easily calmed. Shorty describes Sorrells as "moving so fast his hat was blowed back." He managed well enough "until that old horse turned east and got to jumpin' so high he finally missed the ground." Not long after that episode Sorrells again came upon Northcutt with broncs in the pen, this time four head instead of three.

"Want to try it again?" Northcutt asked.

"One thing about it," Sorrells answered, "the odds are a lot better this time."

Of course, he added, "Shorty gave me my pick the first time, and I reckon I picked the wrong one."

Still, there remained the suspicion that Northcutt knew it was a bad pick and could have warned him off. If so, Sorrells got even with him some time later.

The payback had to do with "a little black horse called Patches" that Sorrells had in his string. He was a good pony under most circumstances, but he had a bad habit of breaking in two and pitching when he'd jump a clump of brush. It was as if the act of jumping reminded him of bucking. Sorrells caught onto the pattern quickly, and made a point to rein away from low brush. It really wasn't a problem except at a dead run, such as when he was trying to turn a cow. Sorrells never had cause to mention the horse's quirk to anyone else, and apparently no one else had noticed it. One day on roundup Northcutt needed a spare mount; his were "all rode down." Sorrells offered him a choice between Patches and another in his string. The alternative, named Angelo, was "a peculiar-movin' kind of old pony," he remembers, and "nobody much liked to ride him."

That included Northcutt, who quickly chose Patches. Sure enough, the horse "took him to a bronc ride" the first time he jumped a bush at a high lope.

Everyone got a chuckle out of the show, but Sorrells took particular delight; Northcutt could pick the wrong pony, too. He enjoyed the episode all over again years later when he finally admitted to Northcutt that it wasn't as pure an accident as it looked at the time.

Fred McClellan cowboyed for Renderbrook in the thirties, and he remembers several Northcutt horse stories. In one, Ted Sorrells was again the victim. It involved a race in which Northcutt had bet Ted that he would "beat him on the jump-off." Shorty was poorly mounted and Sorrells wasn't, so it looked like a cinch to the challengee. He matched the bet to the tune of several hard-to-come-by dollars, and someone called the start. Sorrells was off like a shot, but Northcutt just leaped to the ground and claimed the wager: he'd beaten Sorrells on the "jump-off."

A similar stunt involved a Colorado City man Northcutt described as a "would-be gambler" who was bragging loudly at a rodeo about how fast his horse was. "Hell, I can hold his tail clear across the arena," Northcutt scoffed.

The gambler couldn't pass up a challenge like that and bet Shorty five dollars, a hefty sum in the Depression. Northcutt had a friend mount the "racehorse," took up a position afoot behind the animal, and at the last instant jumped up behind his friend, reached back and grabbed the horse's tail, and away they went. The gambler didn't like being taken, and he sure didn't like being hooted out of the grandstands. He demanded his money back.

"I was gonna' give it to him, too," Northcutt said, until the man got so mad. "After that, I wasn't about to give it back."

McClellan says Northcutt—in addition to his creative out-

Fred McClellan, Ted Sorrells, and Shorty Northcutt reminisce (photo
by Steve Kelton).

look on wagering—"could get more out of a horse than anybody I ever knew." He remembers once when Northcutt won a horse race, then switched mounts with the grumbling loser and beat him again.

Cowboy life wasn't all practical joking. As young, single cowboys, Northcutt and McClellan were teamed in a camp job. And it was, literally, a camp job. The two summered under a brush arbor built to accommodate the crews during the government cow-killing project. Their primary assignment was to treat screwworm cases and, in the process, to educate a string each of green horses.

If the screwworm had any single redeeming quality beyond service to the buzzard population, it was its role in training cowboys and cowponies. Having cow brutes to rope, throw and doctor day in and day out provided horse training of a necessary and practical quality that can never be approached in an arena. For the cowboy, it taught him to throw a loop when the opportunity presented itself; there was a whole world of brush and breaks for his target to get lost and die in, and allowing that to happen carried a cost much higher than an arena roper's wasted entry fee.

Routine work on wormies, of course, created some wrecks of its own. Some were bad ones, but usually their humorous aspects survive the years better than the near-tragedies they also entailed. Northcutt and McClellan were teamed against a cow once when almost nothing seemed to go right. Northcutt was on an "old outlaw" named Salty Dog, McClellan on a horse known as Preacher Brown. Northcutt had the cow by the head but McClellan was having a devil of a time snagging the aft end because Preacher Brown refused to put him in position. Just as McClellan would maneuver his mount into a reasonable facsimile of a proper position, the cow would move and the process would start all over again. Finally, frustrated beyond all endurance, McClellan raised both legs and "jobbed" Preacher Brown with his spurs. The horse responded in kind, launching McClellan up and over, right into a nearby fence.

"He stood on his head and his feet hung in the wire," Northcutt recalls, and the memory brought a belly laugh decades after the event.

After disentangling himself, McClellan remounted and eventually moved into a position that allowed him to capture his end of the wormy cow. Then it was Northcutt's turn to have trouble. Salty Dog "wouldn't work a rope for nothing. You could make him pull but he wouldn't back up a step."

Northcutt became as frustrated with his mount as McClellan had been with his own, but spurs are an improper signal for reverse. Better, Northcutt decided, would be the old chunk of two-by-four lumber he spotted on the ground. He dismounted, picked up the board, "and went to work on his old head." That remedied the situation, but the commotion didn't go unnoticed by Coosey Jackson at the chuckwagon nearby. When Otto Jones stopped by the wagon the next day, Northcutt and McClellan heard Jackson ask in all innocence: "Mr. Jones, ya'll have some new hosses out there? I heard the boys hammerin' some out yesterday."

Even everyday life for Northcutt and McClellan that summer had its interesting aspects, viewed from a distance of a half-century or so. It goes without saying that the duo had no electricity; even if rural electrification had made it deep into Renderbrook by then, which it hadn't, they had no house to electrify. There were, of course, few electrically-powered amenities to miss, outside of refrigeration, and they had that problem solved. The cowboys had dug a hole, lined it with boards, then insulated it with a thick layer of

Branding for an audience, 1932. In the corral (left to right) are Bob McClellan, Pete Ainsworth, Nick Reed, Homer Martin, Jno. Clark and Ray Lane (Southwest Collection, Texas Tech University).

cottonseed hulls. It made an efficient icebox when cooled with hundred-pound blocks of ice. The box was used primarily to keep beef, bacon and eggs—the major components of Northcutt's and McClellan's diets. Frijoles didn't figure in. "We never cooked beans," stressed McClellan. Their breakfast, usually cooked before daylight, was a dozen eggs and a pound of bacon. That had to carry them until about four in the afternoon, when they finished their doctoring rounds and returned to camp.

Then came supper: "a big old steak, onions, pickles and lightbread." They called it a "brush arbor special" and ate it night after night. Their beef, of course, came from Renderbrook, but the remainder of the menu was hauled from town periodically, along with fresh supplies of ice. Northcutt did the hauling in "an old Model A pickup" that he remembers as "so run down you had to pour oil in it every few miles."

McClellan recalls that the old Ford was also as "hard to handle as a cold-jawed horse," a characteristic that contributed to one of the few stories of the period that didn't actually involve a horse. In that particular tale, Northcutt was returning from a grocery run which included a whole tub full of eggs. Coming off a hill and approaching a curve he looked back to check on his supplies "and about that time I run off the road and hit the borrow ditch. All my groceries went together and the ice come down in my eggs."

Horses, however, remained a focal point in their working lives. For a time, the Renderbrook owners raised Arabians on the ranch, and neither Northcutt nor McClellan had a liking for them. One mean stud in particular made horse gathering a miserable and even dangerous chore. There's always a chance that a cowboy and his mount will be attacked if they try to work mares with a stud in residence, but with this "A-rab" stallion it was a dead certainty. One day Northcutt drew the assignment to ride that four-legged terror, so McClellan eared him down and Northcutt stepped aboard. He worked the stud over and in the process lost a spur rowel. The bare shank of that spur clawed the horse's shoulder noticeably, and sure enough, Otto Jones was by the next day.

"What happened to the stud horse?" he asked the crew. Charlie Bloodworth answered for Northcutt: "He run into that fence over yonder."

The cowboys didn't have a lot of favorable things to say about the rest of the Arabians, either. "Most of 'em weren't worth a dime outside of rounding up," Northcutt said. Unlike Quarterhorses or other cow pony breeds and strains, the Arabs hadn't been bred for "cow sense," so they didn't take naturally to the more complex chores like roping, cutting or holding a herd. They have been famous through the ages for their endurance, however, and that made them ideal as drive horses for an outfit like Renderbrook with its big pastures. A man on the outside of a circle, like a youngster on the end of the rope in a game of "crack the whip," might make the entire swing at a lope. An Arabian could hold such a pace long after other horses had dropped out. "You could just run one of 'em all day," Northcutt recalls.

Mules had a reputation for endurance as well, but they were also known for being too smart to run themselves to death. That strong self-preservation instinct was probably one reason some of the non-equestrian Ellwood family members bought a pair of saddle mules for their visits; the mounts might protect their riders while protecting themselves.

Whatever the reason for the mules' presence at Renderbrook, Northcutt was assigned to break them. He remembers one of the two as "pretty good," the other as "just a regular hard-head." Once the rawest edges were off, both Northcutt and McClellan rode the mules. At one time they used them to rustle horses in the morning, Northcutt going out for the remuda one morning on his mule, McClellan going the next day on the other. Northcutt apparently got first pick when the mules were parceled out, because McClellan was stuck with the hard-head.

"One day I heard him just cussin' and ridin'," Northcutt remembers. "Directly he came on in, that mule layin' his ears back. They didn't have any horses."

When the mule and rider arrived, Northcutt discovered that McClellan's bits had broken and the animal was under his own guidance. No matter how vocally he disagreed— and he was doing so vociferously—McClellan had no particular impact on his mount's velocity or direction. But the mules could be entertaining. One cold winter day Northcutt and McClellan were out horseback with nothing in particular to hold their attention or provide enough activity to keep them warm. Actually, Northcutt wasn't riding horseback; he was muleback.

The two hit upon a plan in which McClellan would hide behind a bush and throw his leggings out as Northcutt charged by. The startled mule "just kicked and squealed like a dog," Northcutt recalls. They did it over and over, "and that mule never did get wise to it."

Another Ellwood family mount was a "high-tailed steppin' horse" ridden by one of the Ellwood women. She had had it shipped to the ranch in time for a visit coinciding with roundup work, and rode the stepper out to the wagon and the working grounds. Northcutt was on hand when she rode up, and he recalls that Pete Ainsworth's horse didn't quite know what to make of the strange prancing apparition. It must have looked a little like another horse to him—but not much. Ainsworth was in the middle of the herd cutting cattle out, riding with a typically loose rein to give his cutting horse his head. The animal's first glance at the high-stepper so terrified him that he "ran right back through himself and out the other side of the herd." Ainsworth gathered his reins, jerked the horse around and forced him back, but as soon as he spied the "invader" he was gone again. There was no way Ainsworth could control him until the stepping horse was led away and tied in a brush thicket out of sight.

"Pete still couldn't get anything out of his horse all day long," Northcutt reminisced. "He was always lookin' around. Scared the devil out of him."

Ted Sorrells once had a horse named Ringo in his string, and it would shy at a donkey or Shetland pony. A number of Renderbrook horses, understandably, found sheep to be strange creatures upon first exposure. One was Tom Thumb, from Shorty Northcutt's string. He got his first sight of sheep when Shorty was riding him down a hill at a high lope. "A little bunch of sheep jumped out" of a clump of brush and Tom Thumb did his level best to reverse field. "I'll tell you, I just done everything in the world short of fallin' off," Northcutt says.

Then there was the time the windmill almost threw him. It was the day after Christmas, a holiday not taken lightly by single cowboy revelers, and Northcutt didn't realize just what kind of condition his balance mechanism was in when he started up the tower to grease the mill the morning after. It was one of the old two-tiered wooden towers left over from Eclipse days, a long way from the top to the ground.

Northcutt did well enough climbing the main tower, crossed the big platform and went up the second tower to the motor. Once he'd reached the very top he made the mistake of looking up. He knew not to look down, but hadn't given much thought to any perils from doing the opposite. Clouds were moving doubletime across the sky that morning, however, and to a cowboy suffering the after-effects of too good a time, the illusion was of the tower swaying. "That durn windmill would lean just nearly to the ground," Northcutt recalled, gesturing in a wide arc. "Then it'd come back and go over there. I got ahold of that durn thing and locked my arms around one of the legs . . . I had to shut my eyes. Man, I stayed up there I don't know how long until that spell passed me, then I felt my way off. I wasn't about to open my eyes, and I never was able to climb a windmill after that."

Other than on special occasions, drinking was generally frowned upon on most ranches, Renderbrook no exception. Cowboys most places observed the rule well enough but still managed to put a little firewater away when they wanted to. Northcutt and McClellan remember the aftermath of one short drive to the rail pens at Iatan. They'd finished loading several hundred head of cull cows and bulls evidently purchased from Renderbrook by W. L. Ellwood's trading partner, Len McClellan (no relation to Fred). McClellan was on hand to watch the loading, which was not accomplished that day without some difficulty and delay.

"I'd give anything for a drink of whiskey," he told the crew, each and every member of which agreed without hesitation.

Prohibition was in full swing, but Shorty knew of a local bootlegger, so McClellan gave him "$10 or $15" to buy spirits for the men. Whatever the exact figure, it paid for a gallon of moonshine, enough to get the crew plenty good-spirited.

Otto Jones' brother Fred was among them, and Fred McClellan remembered Jones driving the saddle horses back to Renderbrook afterward. "One of those horses turned off on him," McClellan recalls, "and old Fred started out to head him. He was going pretty fast when all of a sudden a covey of quail flushed right under his horse. He just reached out and grabbed one, caught that thing in flight.

"If he'd drank a little more," McClellan said with mock solemnity, "he might have caught two."

Otto, however, was seldom seen to drink. In fact it surprised the cowboys when he did. Fred McClellan said the only time he ever saw Otto Jones "let his hair down" around the full crew was once at Smyer when they had finished loading a large shipment of calves off the Spade destined for Fort Worth. Jones had driven there in his car and was going to ride on to Fort Worth on the train, so he had arranged to leave the car in a garage at the pens. The crew was gathered in the garage to bed down, Jones among them. Otto asked Northcutt to "get me that corn medicine from my bag over there."

Northcutt took him literally and reached down to comply, looking for some sort of concoction to use on sore feet. There was none, just a bottle of whiskey.

"Of course, I didn't bother that," he remembers. "I said, 'I don't see any corn medicine.'"

"Yes, you do," Jones answered, retrieving the corn-based "medicine" himself. After a long pull he gave the bottle to the cowboys to finish.

Along with bootlegged liquor, during Prohibition the cowboys were known to drink grain alcohol, diluted and sugared. Drinking, however, was much more of a diversion, even a game, than a habit with the general run of cowboys despite popular perceptions to the contrary. Cow sense, performance and attention to duty were matters of intense pride to most cowhands; allowing alcohol or any other habit to interfere with those attributes was viewed as shameful.

The thirties marked a transition not only for the cowboys but also for Renderbrook's owners as the next generation of I. L. Ellwood's heirs had their first contact with the Texas holdings. W. L. Ellwood's daughter Jessie—alias Jean—during the decade of the teens had met and married Frank H. Chappell of New London, Connecticut. The Chappell family owned the Thames Tugboat Company on Connecticut's Thames River, as well as the Chappell Coal and Lumber Company. Frank Chappell was the brother of one of Jessie's classmates at Mary Burnham School in Northhampton, Massachusetts, and she met him on a visit to the Chappell home.[2] Their children were Marion, born in 1918, and Frank, Jr., born in 1920.

The Chappell children lived a comfortable New England coastal life through their early childhoods, but the pattern took an abrupt turn about 1935 when the family paid a visit to Texas. The precise date is uncertain, but Marion remembers the "new" bunkhouse being under construction at the time; it was built in 1935. Despite fuzziness about the date, other details remain sharply in her memory.[3]

The trip by train took "the best part of three days and two nights," and the Chappells arrived in Colorado City after dark. Otto Jones, Pete Ainsworth and another cowboy met them in two pickups. Marion and her parents rode back with Jones, Frank, Jr., with Ainsworth and the other hand. Ainsworth struck out in the lead, and by the time they arrived at the old stone arch marking the ranch entrance off the Colorado City-Sterling City road, they had pulled far out of sight of Jones. The cowboys stopped at the arch, opened the door and let young Frank out in the dark.

"This is as far as we go," one of them told him. "You just wait here and the rest of 'em will be along directly."

They had, of course, fed him liberally on stories of rattlesnakes and other dangerous creatures during the drive.

He made his first step toward acceptance among the cowboys when he took them at their word and disembarked despite the scare tactics. Ainsworth and his co-conspirator laughed and drove Frank on in to headquarters.

His sister Marion never forgot her first impression of Renderbrook in the early-morning light. "You look off and you don't see the end of anything. It's just big, and the land rolls on and on. I just fell in love with the place." She returned as often as possible in the next few years, at first with her parents and later on her own when their schedules didn't accommodate the frequency or length of visits she desired.

"Sometimes I'd just say, 'I'm going to stay with Otto.'" The young heiress fell into the Renderbrook routine more deeply than many native Texas ranch women. "I sure did like to get up in the black of the morning and go with the boys to wherever they were going to round up. At dinnertime sometimes the other ladies would come out, but I just loved to ride. I think those boys were very tolerant to let me go along every time, too, because there I was, a female."

It undoubtedly put a crimp in some of their language, anecdotes and practical jokes, but she appears to have been well accepted by the Renderbrook hands. They even took her to town with them on Saturday nights. Standard procedure was to take in a movie and a cafe meal.

"In those days that was pretty important; now you can go to town whenever you want to and it doesn't seem like anything at all."

To Marion, however, the really important times were those she spent on the ranch itself, particularly in the early years.

"Those big roundups—I shall never forget them. The sound of the cows lowing, some of the old ones sounding like squeaky door hinges. I got to know pretty much how they separated them into groups to sell some, and the keeping heifers. What an uproar it is all night when they separate the cows from their first calves," she recalls. The ruckus was hard to sleep through sometimes, "but you know, you get to liking it.

"I'm glad I can remember that because it seemed that kind of living just went by in a hurry. We didn't have the telephone or electricity on the ranch until I'd been married a couple of years. We used kerosene lanterns for light, and if somebody wanted to tell you something they'd have to come down and talk to you. I thoroughly enjoyed living that way, and it was a great place for kids."

One of her prized possessions of those years was her first saddle. She had been using one of the ranch's spares on her visits until it became apparent that her obsession with Renderbrook and cowboying was to be a chronic affliction. Finally her mother sent money to buy her a saddle of her own. "I was down at the pens working sheep," she said, when Otto Jones decided it was time to make the purchase. He apparently just intended to consult with her and then choose the saddle himself, but Marion insisted on picking it out.

"I wouldn't think of not going with him. Mrs. Jones said, 'Well, look at you, you're all dirty.' I said, 'that's all right, I'll wash my face and hands,' and by gosh that's what I did. I went with them that very day, and we went down to M. L. Leddy's. Oh, I was so excited. Mrs. Jones and the others laughed at me because I just had to take off as dirty as I was and go to San Angelo to buy that saddle."

Memorable events back home in Connecticut ranged from the family's annual tugboat picnic trip to watch the Harvard-Yale sculling race at New London to trips to New York for a night at the opera. At Renderbrook the big event was Colorado City's annual fall rodeo. "Everybody wanted to be in the parade," Marion recalls, so local cowboys would all bring a horse to town. Marion would usually go with the Joneses and their two daughters, Frances and Polly. Festivities continued for several days.

And when there was no event, there was still an invigorating life with a tremendous contrast to that in New England. "Here we've got deer and antelope, all sorts of wildlife, and rattlesnakes—I'd never been introduced to a rattlesnake before."

She was never a particularly enthusiastic hunter herself, except when it came to rattlesnakes and jackrabbits. Marion has a picture of "a Packard, I think," with running boards that were often loaded down on summer evenings with armed cowboys.

"In the evenings after supper we'd go out in that old car and shoot rabbits. You know sometimes the rabbit population gets so numerous that they overrun everything else. We would have guns sticking out all the windows, shooting rabbits. Nannie, one of my aunts, said, 'Ya'll look just like the Deadwood stage.'"

Marion had her own horse at Renderbrook, a black and white paint she called Pretty Thing. He was a ranch horse until her mother got wind of an interest her cousin I. L., Jr., and his wife Marjorie had shown in taking Pretty Thing for their son, Perry.

"She went up in smoke," Marion said. She paid Renderbrook for the horse, "and got Will Eisenberg to make a deed of sale."

Pretty Thing carried her through a string of roundups, most of them conducted under typically clear, dry skies but a few in the driving rain.

"They usually could tell if there was going to be weather, but I remember sometimes it would get to raining so hard that the mud was just like pudding under your horse's feet.

That old clay gets really slippery." That was particularly true, she recalls, at the Peter L pens along the Colorado. "Everything would get so muddy that if you had the cattle in the pens you'd have to turn them out again and wait until the next day. Trucks couldn't get down there to load them out or anything." Marion missed the trail drive era, but she remembers one short drive to the railroad at Colorado City. "We'd go by a farm and the housewife would come out to be sure the cows didn't run over her fence and into her garden."

Otto Jones, on the other hand, "would worry that she might booger the cows and stampede them in the wrong direction." Shorty Northcutt once suggested that farmers along the route between Renderbrook and the Colorado City rail pens actually welcomed the herds. "We'd strip some of their cotton," he explained, "but Jones would go up and reimburse 'em, and they'd always get about three times what their cotton was worth."[4] Paying a farm wife for what she thinks her vegetable garden is worth—now that's a different matter. Stories of Marion's Texas experiences amazed and delighted friends in Connecticut, though some of the anecdotes may have been a bit gritty for New England tastes. She once told "a doctor friend" back home about a cow having difficulty calving, and about pulling the calf with a pickup. "She thought that sounded pretty rough."

Eventually some of her friends came to Renderbrook to see for themselves. They were on a cross-country car trip— a major adventure in itself as late as the thirties and forties—and worked a West Texas leg into their itinerary. "They stopped at the ranch and stayed with us for awhile, and they have never forgotten that trip."

Among the visitors' experiences was a first-hand lesson in the changeability of Texas weather. One of the girls "got so sunburned she practically made herself sick," and during the same visit another chilled down to the point that cowboy Joe Boatwright had to loan her a coat. Joe "had been chewing tobacco and the coat kinda' smelled bad. It made her sick, but we all had fun."

Marion trained as a nurse in Connecticut, but her attention was drawn more and more to Texas as the years passed. Various cowboys caught her eye during those years, but Renderbrook's head windmiller, B. D. "Dee" Bassham, managed to catch and hold it. They were married in Lubbock in 1946, after Bassham's return from service in World War II. If anyone had any concerns that marrying an heir to the ranch might go to Bassham's head, they needn't have worried. Pete Ainsworth's wife, Marguerite, visiting with the newlyweds during their wedding reception in a Lubbock hotel, counseled them to have a nice honeymoon.

"Oh, I don't know," Marion recalls her new husband saying, "there are a lot of windmills that need work." Sure enough, they spent at least part of their honeymoon visiting various Spade divisions. One place they didn't go right away was Connecticut, and in fact Marion made few return trips to her hometown during her married life.

"Dee went with us one time to Connecticut," she explained, "and he said, 'once is enough.' We got up there and all these little roads went this way and that with all the traffic. He said, 'this is all very interesting, but we don't need to do it again.'"

Dee Bassham was a Texan by birth and a West Texan by choice, coming out from the eastern part of the state with his father at a young age. He worked for a time in California and Washington, and he ranged as far from home as North Africa in the service. He took his family on regular summer vacations to Colorado and once to California and Oregon. By most standards he would qualify as pretty well traveled,

but he always preferred West Texas, especially Renderbrook.

"We were just happy where we were," explains Marion.
The newlyweds bounced from house to house, camp to
camp on Renderbrook the first few years as Otto Jones jug-
gled various ranch families seeking optimum distribution.
If it ever occured to them to "pull rank," they apparently
didn't give the notion much thought. "It seemed like we
were always moving around, but then all the cowboys
did," recalls Marion. "I thoroughly enjoyed it."

Marion and Dee raised two sons and a daughter, Frank,
Brian and Ida Jean. In the mid-sixties, when they reached
an age where "they didn't need Momma to take them to
PTA and things," Marion decided to put her nursing training to good use. She went to work at the hospital in Colorado City, retiring only after nearly twenty years. By then
she had grandchildren to enjoy, but she kept a hand in
among the medical community by serving on the hospital
board. "I've always been interested in hospitals, even when
I was small. I always wanted to be a nurse," she explained.

Dee Bassham passed away in the spring of 1971. In describing her late husband to a visitor who had never known
him, Marion summed him up fondly as an outdoor enthu-
siast "and a wonderful daddy."

Frank, Jr., also took to the ranch with considerable relish.
When he'd had all the higher education he felt he could
safely hold, Frank slipped his hobbles and moved to Renderbrook. Once there, despite his status as heir, Otto Jones
put him to work. He wasn't long out of Connecticut and
still green as a gourd when butchering time rolled around
and the cowboys offered him the honor of killing the chosen beef. The procedure varied from outfit to outfit, some
employing a gun, others stunning a roped and tied animal
with a sledge hammer or the backside of a single-bit axe,

then winching it up and bleeding it out before it could come to. The Renderbrook hands solemnly provided Frank Chappell with a length of two-inch pipe and instructed him to hit the old cow a good lick with it.

"She just looked puzzled when I hit her," Chappell recalled. "They had a lot of fun with me out there."[5]

Twenty years later, in the presence of Otto Jones and Joe Christopher, an old cowman he had known all that time, Chappell made some routine observation of range condition or cow quality. The remark has long since been forgotten, but not the dry response it elicited from Christopher.

"You know, Otto," Christopher said, gesturing to the by then nearly middle-aged Chappell, "that boy is beginning to notice things."

His carefree cowboy period lasted until he joined the service in World War II. As young Frank was leaving to go overseas, Otto Jones took him aside for a personal goodbye and gave him a special good luck talisman to bring him home safely. The gift was a Spade tie-tack, one of several Frank's mother had had made in New York decades earlier as presents for the cowboys who had accompanied her on her only trail drive from Renderbrook to the Plains ranch. Every hand received one except the cook. "She didn't like him and neither did anyone else," Chappell explains.

Jones had worn that tie-tack proudly on each of his relatively few dress occasions over the years, and Frank knew how much he treasured it. He vowed to himself that he would return it, a promise he would have to come home to keep.

Whether or not that little Spade tie-bar had anything to do with it, Frank Chappell did return. Then he was faced with carrying out the second half of his vow—returning the gift to a friend who wasn't in the habit of taking back things he'd given away. Frank finally hit on the solution. He sent the tie-tack back to Tiffany's, the famous jewelry firm that had made it in the first place, with an order to duplicate it. To his delight the copy was exact right down to dents and dings that the original had accumulated over the years. Telling Jones he'd never looked quite complete without his tie-tack, Frank explained about having had a copy made, and he presented the ranch manager what he assured him was the copy. It wasn't until years after Jones' death that Frank Chappell admitted he had kept the copy himself and given the original back to its rightful owner.

"It brought me home," he explained. "That's what it was supposed to do."

Frank again took up residence at Renderbrook after the war, bringing his new bride, Marcia. In time the couple moved to Lubbock, where Frank turned his hand in part to sharing in Spade management decisions, working alongside W. F. Eisenberg. The Chappells were to remain in Lubbock for twenty years, raising a daughter, Jenny, and two sons, Robert and Frank, III. Among other civic accomplishments, Frank Chappell was a prime mover in establishing the Ranching Heritage Center at Texas Tech, where authentic ranch buildings are grouped and furnished just as they were when in use. Included in the unique living history exhibit is the old Renderbrook blacksmith shop.[6]

In the early 1970s the Chappells retired to Waterford, Connecticut, moving in next door to Frank's boyhood home.

Clouds of War,
None of Rain

T HE CLOSE OF THE 1930s brought
an end to the transition between the pioneer era, which was
characterized by practices left over and little changed from
free range days, and its successor, a time heavily influenced
by and dependent upon the modern machine age. Ranching during the 1940s bowed to the undeniable realities of a
shortage of skilled labor when the United States went to
war. As they had in Teddy Roosevelt's day, cowboys were
among the first to cut loose and throw in with the military
in World War II. They weren't strangers to physical danger
and open-air accommodations, and the single men, at least,
had a footloose and fancy-free tradition to uphold. Sadly,
the conflict swallowed up large numbers of cowboys, married and unmarried, who never came home from the bat-
tlefields.

Renderbrook was fortunate not to lose any of its men to
combat, though a highly regarded hand named Jernigan
disappeared in northern California after the war ended. His

car and personal effects were found, but he was never seen or heard from again. Still, the ranch was critically short-handed for the duration, with more than a half-dozen permanent cowboys serving in uniform. "All we could get was kids," Shorty Northcutt remembers. "We just had to get by as best we could."[1]

Ranching during that time, like most other industries, was in a holding pattern. Coping meant learning new ways of doing things to compensate for what was at first naively expected to be a short period of inconvenience. Everyone agreed that the boys would be back before long.

Everyone was wrong. Unlike the relatively brief war of Teddy Roosevelt, cousin Franklin's conflict dragged on and on, and its grasp spread wide. When it was finally over, a large share of an entire generation of young men lay buried in scattered cemeteries across the globe. Many others had had all the excitement they wanted and came home with a burning desire to settle down with old sweethearts if they were still available, new ones if not. Having experienced first-hand the fragility of life, many young cowboys were older than their days and were ready to raise a family and leave the fighting and the intense camraderie of the service behind. Four years of war altered forever the face of ranching. With fairly rare exceptions, the cowboys who came home soon brought brides with them. If there was no place for the women, the hands would stay no longer.

Many cowboys never came all the way back, at least not to the ranch. New skills, new opportunities through such programs as the GI Bill, or simply a broadened awareness of what wonders lay beyond the ranch fence sidetracked many cowhands before they made it back to the bunkhouse.

In West Texas, one of the wonders beyond barbed wire was the burgeoning oil and gas industry.

Renderbrook had its first brush with the petroleum industry in 1929 when the Sims Oil Company moved a rig within two miles of headquarters and began "putting down hole" toward a 3000-foot wildcat oil well. The crew struck an unexpected gas pocket at about 600 feet, and before they could get the well shut in their rig had burned to the ground. Undaunted—perhaps encouraged, in fact—the oil men moved over a ways from the first hole and deliberately drilled for natural gas. With that well to provide fuel, and thereby reduce drilling costs, they went back in and completed their wildcat.[2]

After all that trouble, however, the oil well turned out to be a dry hole. The company had a gas well, of course, but at such a shallow depth it clearly would never be a big producer, and it took considerable production to justify the cost of a gathering system for gas. Even major fields in those days routinely flared off their gas byproduct; the torches burned around the clock, giving the night an eerie twilight quality in many areas of West Texas. That didn't happen to the Renderbrook gas well. W. L. Ellwood bought out the oil company's rights to it and piped its output to headquarters. Long before the ranch enjoyed commercial electricity it could boast of gas heating, cooking and even refrigeration.[3] And the well whose production was too scant to have commercial value was still serving Renderbrook's needs more than sixty years later.

Like any other breed of gambler, the oil wildcatter tends to remember successes long after failures are forgotten. That the first Renderbrook hole was a duster didn't count as much as the fact that it at least spewed gas, and the oilmen overlooked the second, third and many more such dusters in the next few years. The rancher's certainty that each passing day in a drouth carries him one day closer to rain is mirrored in the oilman's apparent conviction that each dry

Working cattle on the Plains (Spade Ranches Collection); *below, crew and owners at the chuckwagon* (Southwest Collection, Texas Tech University). *Both photos were taken in the fall of 1942.*

hole is one step nearer the payoff. They took a lot of those steps on Renderbrook in the late 1930s and through the forties. Jones recalled the usual lease price being three to four dollars per acre as a bonus with an annual renewal fee of fifty cents. The drillers' optimism eventually paid off when oil began to flow from Renderbrook in the early 1950s.

Frank Chappell recalled W. F. Eisenberg's reaction to news that the first well had come in. Eisenberg leaned back in his desk chair, tipped his hat back, and gestured with his ever-present cigar to Chappell and others in the Lubbock office at the time. "Boys," he intoned with mock solemnity, "if we're careful I think we can run fifty cows to the well."[4]

Before long there would be scores of such oil wells, mostly on the back side of Renderbrook, across the Coke County line in the Silver area.[5] They provided a "mineral supplement," at last easing the financial pinch that had for so long squeezed the Spade operation. The oil peak would last only a few short years before it began a long and as-yet uncompleted decline, but the financial boon wrapped up a lot of loose ends that had been dangling for decades.

It also helped Renderbrook and the Spades through their next trying period. The "Drouth," as it came to be called, began as early as 1949 in the semi-desert country of Southwest Texas. From there it eased gradually north and east in an age-old pattern that was probably as recognizable and predictable as it was unrecognized and unpredicted. The new decade was a year or two underway before ranchers and farmers in West Texas began to realize that the increasing dryness around them was something out of the ordinary. Then, the worse it got the nearer most operators figured they were to the end of it. Drouths always ended; the trick was to outlast them. Many producers outlasted the fifties Drouth with little more left than their lives, and more

W. F. Eisenberg, late 1950s (Spade Ranches Collection).

than a few fared worse still, working and worrying themselves into an early grave before the rains came.

As bad as the Dust Bowl drouth of the 1930s was, it can claim no better than second place against the seven-year dry spell that dominated the 1950s. Not that it didn't rain at all for seven years; the rains were simply too seldom, too light and too scattered.

One of the first casualties at Renderbrook was the sheep program. As the Drouth deepened, the managers found their original set of sheep-fenced pastures overgrazed.[6] The natural response was to string more net wire in new areas, but that plan quickly ran into serious snags. It was one thing to fence a piece of ground and call it a pasture, quite another to utilize it as one, particularly when water was scarce. Otto Jones recalled that most of the new sheep pastures relied on dirt tanks for stock water, and that the tanks were suffering drouth stress right along with the rangeland. As water in the tanks receded in ever-dwindling pools at the center, more and more of the old deeply silted bottoms became exposed. These might bear a crust of dry dirt, but under the crust often lay deep bogs of fresh mud. Where a cow might manage to flounder out of such a trap, a bogged sheep was usually there until it died or was rescued; between wet wool and a natural tendency to simply give up, sheep more often than not came out second best in a battle with the mud.

"That pretty well helped us decide to get out of the sheep business," Jones said.[9] Renderbrook shipped the remainder of its sheep in 1952, three years short of two decades from the time their forebears first arrived. The ranch would run sheep again; the economics were just too good not to, given a reasonable chance. The woollies didn't return until the 1960s, however, after the Drouth had played itself out and the land's wounds had healed a bit.[8]

By then Renderbrook had for several years been strictly a concern of the Chappell side of the family. Most of Perry Ellwood's share of the land and real property contained in Isaac Ellwood's estate was apparently taken from Illinois holdings when the estate was finally closed late in the thirties. The only Texas land conveyed to Perry Ellwood's heirs at his death six days into 1943 was the "HS" ranch unit bordering Renderbrook on the south and west. That left Renderbrook and the remaining Spade acreage on the Plains in the hands of W. L.'s heirs, Jean (Jessie) Chappell and Elise (Harriet) Keeney.[9] With the experience of the long, drawn-out Isaac Ellwood estate closing sharp in his recent memory, W. F. Eisenberg could see the wisdom in divvying up W. L.'s legacy quickly and cleanly.

That would help ward off situations like the one that ensnarled the two estates for a time in 1934 over a loan on 4000 head of cattle taken out from Texas Production Credit Association by W. L. several months before his death.[10] W. L. sold the cattle to the I. L. Ellwood estate in July of 1933, and that entity made a payment on the short-term note when it came due. With cash tight, the Ellwoods chose to maintain the loan as long as they held the cattle. That posed no problem until after W. L. himself passed away that December; when Eisenberg sought to renew the original loan in the late W. L.'s name the following spring, lawyers and lending officials balked. They declined to renew a loan to the W. L. Ellwood estate on cattle that belonged to the I. L. Ellwood estate, despite the fact that the transfer had occurred at least one renewal earlier, the latter estate had actually been making note payments all along, and the same individuals were in charge of both estates.

It should have been no problem. The old note could simply have been retired—as one attorney suggested—in favor of a new one in the name of I. L.'s estate, had not the lawyers stumbled onto a zinger in their perusal of Isaac Ellwood's will. According to the terms of that instrument, the estate was to have been settled in a maximum of ten years. As interpreted by Charles Gibbs, attorney for the Regional Agricultural Credit Corporation, that meant the executors of I. L.'s estate had been "without authority to act since 1920."

That discrepancy had raised its head before, so the estate lawyers had a ready solution. For the purposes of the Production Credit note, Perry Ellwood's signature was required as executor of both the Isaac and W. L. Ellwood estates, and as an individual heir of the former. In addition, Eisenberg had to sign as the other W. L. Ellwood estate executor. Finally, the PCA required releases from every other I. L. Ellwood heir, just in case Perry Ellwood's trusteeship was indeed invalid. It was certainly not a smooth way to run a business that depended upon borrowed money and the routine buying and selling of chattel property.

Eisenberg could not have wanted to go through the experience again, and with the final separation of the brothers' affairs following Perry's death, he moved as quickly as possible to close the W. L. Ellwood Estate. The first step was an agreement between Jean and Elise to divide their Renderbrook and Spade properties.

On June 4, 1948, Elise Keeney deeded her half-interest in roughly 63,000 acres on the east side of Renderbrook to Jean Chappell in exchange for Jean's previously undivided half interest in just under 58,000 acres on the west side.[11] The sisters had already divided the remaining 60,000 acres of Spade land in the Panhandle, and Elise had sold her 30,000 acre share to a farmland syndicate for cash to purchase the headquarters and 130,000 acres of the historic old Bell Ranch in San Miguel County, New Mexico. The Chappells bought an additional 40,000 acres of Bell Ranch land, but without disposing of any of their Spade acreage.[13]

The situation changed entirely in the mid-1950s when the Keeneys exchanged their half of Renderbrook for the 30,000 acres of Spade land held by the Chappells, switching the last of the old Spade to Keeney family hands and leaving the Chappell side of the family with sole ownership of Renderbrook.[13]

At the time, Renderbrook might have seemed more like a liability than an asset. The fortuitous discovery of oil on Renderbrook helped the Spades survive the Drouth, but for cowboys and cowmen it was a depressing decade. Shorty Northcutt describes the period as "dull and uninteresting" on Renderbrook; with its mineral income the ranch was freed of any necessity to try to tough it out with its cow herd, so the vast majority of the cattle were shipped early in the period. Many of the better cows initially went to a ranch the outfit leased near Lamesa. "They just kept enough cows at Renderbrook for seed," Northcutt recalls.[14]

When the cows left, so did most of the hands, including Northcutt, who picked that unlikely time to go into the cattle business for himself. The only regular cowmen who remained during the period, in addition to Otto Jones, were Shim Swann, Ted Sorrells and Wright Hock. Their days, winter and summer, became a monotonous routine of feeding and checking waterings. The skeleton herd that remained was given the run of Renderbrook's big pastures, where it was hoped they would find enough to eat to get them by from one feed run to the next. An obvious drawback to the arrangement was that it became hard to feed such a scattered herd. Eventually the cost of gasoline added to that of overpriced sack feed forced the ranch to limit its charity to the cows that came handy. It was just too expensive to hunt the others up.

And it became even more expensive. Long before the Drouth was over, Renderbrook found itself feeding animals hay as well as grain and protein.[15] On native West Texas range, that is considered an extreme practice and a sure sign of impending bankruptcy for most operators. The government finally stepped in to help, but the kind of assistance it provided soured many a rancher on the entire concept of government aid.

One well-intentioned emergency feed program was rushed into operation before the rules governing it could be drafted. To speed relief, cooperators were urged to act quickly and many did. To their dismay they soon discovered that federal bureaucrats had written rules after the fact outlawing much of what had been done out of necessity and in good faith under emergency conditions. While suppliers of spoiled or otherwise unusable feed were reaping hefty government checks, honest men often found their legitimate claims refused for failure to comply with pointless regulations. More than a few were held liable for penalties. A more straightforward program directly subsidized feed purchases, allowing $10 per ton on hay, for instance. Overnight, of course, hay prices went up to the full $10, sometimes more. This was a boon to some feed suppliers but did stockmen no good and actually penalized those who declined to take government money.

The long dry spell seemed like a permanent fixture by early 1957 when the Chappell, Bassham and Keeney families decided to lighten the somber mood a bit. As the fiftieth anniversary of Otto Jones' employment with the Spades neared, the owners began putting together a surprise celebration not only for Jones but also for Spade manager Tom Arnett and W. F. Eisenberg. Marion Bassham worked on the Colorado City end of the gathering as brother Frank ramrodded the preparations that were handled from Lubbock. It was not to be a garden-variety barbecue; the co-conspirators consulted the honorees' wives, relatives and friends to draw up an all-inclusive guest list, then mailed literally hundreds of invitations to people all over the country. Fully 400 relatives, neighbors, livestock buyers and former Spade cowboys were to show up for the affair, including a one-time hand from as far away as Wyoming. A crowd that size was far beyond the capacity of a chuck-wagon cook to handle, so the barbecue was catered, served under the ancient walnut trees around Renderbrook Spring.[16]

It was no small job coordinating all the arrangements, and it was made all the harder by the fact that Jones and Eisenberg were right in the middle of things while the planning and preparations were underway. There was no way to keep the project a secret from the two honorees, so the planners didn't try. Instead, they put the men to work. Jones was told that the effort was geared to hosting the annual meeting of Texas and Southwestern Cattle Raisers Association field inspectors. And it was, sort of; the lawmen had indeed been invited to conduct their get-together at Renderbrook that late-summer weekend, in large measure to provide just such a cover for the real party. There simply wasn't any way to keep Jones in the dark, so upper-level management had to fool him with the diversion instead. Eisenberg, who may have been the most surprised of all when he turned out to be an honoree, was also included in the conspiracy. He was in on the scheme from the beginning, or thought he was. From helping to coordinate the guest list to arranging catering and transportation, Eisenberg had a hand in everything. The one thing he didn't know was that he was planning his own party as well as theirs.

And Mother Nature surprised everyone. Not long into

Tom Arnett, Otto Jones, W. F. Eisenberg, Frank Chappell, Jr., at the 1957 celebration (Spade Ranches Collection).

the party she treated the hosts, honorees and guests to a hard shower that sent them scurrying to houses, barns and sheds. The first drouth-breaking rains had come months earlier, but the shower that freshened the barbecue served as a reminder that the seven-year Drouth was really over.

Fast-Paced Change

11

W<small>HEN</small> the serious rains finally returned, they came with a vengeance, as if nature were trying to make up for her parsimony or perhaps to destroy with flooding what little she had failed to parch and blow away.

It began raining in early March of 1957, about a month after President Dwight D. Eisenhower passed through West Texas on a drouth tour. The rangeland rebounded almost overnight, sprouting greenery from stores of weed and grass seed laid back in good years of long before. Tens of thousands of dirt tanks that were bone dry or boggy one day were brimful and running the next, and the timing of the rains was such that spring green-up seemed almost as rapid.

There weren't enough cows, sheep or goats in the whole country to restock the suddenly verdant pastures, but few ranchers could have afforded them had they been available and fewer still would have bought back to full strength had they been both available and affordable. The Drouth had been far too intense an experience to shake off that quickly, and some operators held back and let grass go to waste well after they were capable of stocking to utilize it. Seven years of drouth burned so deep in a rancher's subconscious that it became nearly instinctive to look for a dust storm instead of a thunderstorm whenever the wind shifted directions.

Renderbrook restocked as rapidly as was practical, but much of the ranch's infrastructure was badly deteriorated by Drouth's end. Many old fences, corrals and waterings had passed the end of their useful lives during the long dry spell and, unneeded, had gone unrepaired by the short-handed crew. When the rains returned and cattle with them, these long-idle structures were once again in demand.[1] To help with the rebuilding, Otto Jones sought out Shorty Northcutt. Operating his own ranch prudently and pinching pennies where he could, Northcutt had managed to come out of the Drouth with more than he had when he went into it. That was better than a lot of outfits had done, but he was still feeling the financial strain enough to listen attentively to Jones' proposal.

"He offered me too much to turn down," Northcutt recalled in later years. Perhaps equally important, however, Jones was offering a position as assistant manager. Included was responsibility and authority for making changes where Northcutt deemed necessary. "He was offering me a chance to improve a ranch. It was what I'd wanted to do all my life. I'd be doing it for somebody else, but I'd finally get to do it." Like Uncle Dick Arnett long decades before, Northcutt kept his private ranching interests on the side, but he came back to Renderbrook. His head was swimming with plans and ideas, most of which had to wait while a more pressing problem dominated that first wet spring and summer.

"Screwworms like to have eaten us up," he remembered clearly. "We doctored every durn head on the ranch before that spell was over." In time the worms let up and Render-brook could get on with other things.

With his own experiences during the Drouth to guide him, Northcutt instituted some economies he could see were badly needed. One of the first was to eliminate the old cow-country custom of eating fresh beef. Renderbrook, like most of the other cow outfits of any size, had gotten into the habit decades earlier of killing a beef at regular inter-vals. They would start with the choicest parts and consume whatever they could while it was still fresh, then discard the rest and kill another animal. By the time Northcutt put a stop to it, the custom was costing the ranch about a beef a week. What finally brought the magnitude of waste home to him was looking at all the parts of carcasses rotting in the outfit's dump pit. It hadn't seemed so extravagant when there were enough mouths on Renderbrook to consume an entire beef before it spoiled, and there really hadn't been a good alternative. By the late fifties, however, the ranch was so thinly populated that the bones going into the dump still had a lot of meat on them. This time there was an alterna-tive: Northcutt bought freezers for headquarters residences and all the occupied camps. Slaughter for home consump-tion plummeted to three or four head a year.

He also put into effect some stock-working economies that represented significant capital investments initially, but like the freezers would pay off year after year. Among the largest projects of that sort was a fencing program that cut the remaining big pastures into smaller enclosures of a half-dozen or so sections at most. These would later be reduced even further, but the first cross-fences greatly sim-plified cow work, eliminating the big roundups that re-quired large crews and went for days at a stretch, rain or shine. Similarly, working pens within reach of each pasture did away with the need for manpower to hold a herd and a "cut" out in the open. Scales and loading facilities further mechanized things, but one of Northcutt's proudest accomplishments on Renderbrook was the brush control program.

"I made a statement once that I've since thought I ought to have taken back," he recalled. The crew had just finished a roundup drive through a brushy pasture, and irritation at the unnecessary difficulty of the job was fresh in his mind when Northcutt told a reporter: "If I had to give up screwworm control or brush control, I would give up screwworm control. I could handle the screwworms without brush better than I can handle the brush."[2]

He later decided he didn't mean the part about giving up screwworm control, at least not literally. But that bold statement did pretty accurately reflect his feelings about brush control.

"Brush control is the greatest thing since wheels were invented," he told the same reporter, and he never expressed second thoughts about that assertion. Brush encroachment over the years had made Renderbrook a considerably less productive and conveniently operated piece of land than it had been when Isaac and W. L. Ellwood made their first buggy tour in 1889. The earliest travelers through the country sought out camping sites near creeks and draws even when they had their own water; these sheltered areas had been the only places where firewood could be readily found. Continuous grazing and suppression of range fires soon began to change that. Mesquite, catclaw, cedar and other brush species crept slowly out of their age-old niches and spread to some of the best grazing land. Their demand for water sapped moisture from the grass, and as competition from the grass weakened, the brush grew more prolific still.

Testimony to its severity, the Drouth itself killed some mesquites, but by far the greatest majority of the brush killed on Renderbrook was done deliberately and at considerable cost. The first method attempted was cabling, using a heavy oilfield cable and a bulldozer to drag brush down. Chaining followed in the sixties, a similar technique except that a massive ship's anchor chain replaced the cable.[3]

These methods, unless followed up with a burn or other mechanical cleanup, leave rangeland badly littered with fallen timber, sometimes making it as hard to work through as it had been when the brush was standing. Their biggest drawback, however, is that they usually provide only a temporary top-kill to such tenacious resprouting species as mesquite. Sooner or later—most often sooner—the plant will be back with eight or ten stems where the single trunk had been, and the well-developed root system of the mature plant to feed the new tops. Some veteran brush fighters insist that top-killing actually stimulates the unwanted invaders, like pruning a neglected shade tree. Renderbrook was one of the first ranches to attempt herbicidal mesquite control, initially in an effort to control resprouting in previously cabled or chained pastures. In time they began to focus the spraying effort on original growth, skipping the knockdown phase. The ranch has remained in the forefront of brush control experimentation and demonstrations ever since, including hosting controlled burning demonstrations at least as early as 1968.[4] Few ranchers at that time could conceive of the terms "controlled" and "burning" in the same sentence.

Rebuilding after the Drouth occupied several years and wasn't fully in hand by Northcutt's reckoning until 1962 or '63. By then an ominous cloud of an entirely different sort had swept in. Death struck first on February 13, 1962, with the passing of Frank Chappell, Sr., and swept several other lives off the Renderbrook-Spade roster before it was finished. Leland Keeney was next, dying September 18, 1963, and Mrs. Perry Ellwood, "Aunt May" to Marion and Frank, Jr., followed December 17, 1964.[5]

On the first day of November, 1965, Renderbrook's ownership passed to a new generation with the death of Jean Chappell. Unlike the direct line of descent the ranch had followed from I. L. Ellwood to W. L. and Perry and from W. L. to Jean and Elise, ownership this time bowed to the realities of the tax man. At W. F. Eisenberg's urging, Jean Chappell skipped Marion and Frank and passed Renderbrook to their children. The parents would enjoy a life estate and management authority, but ownership was vested directly in the next generation to escape one slice of the tax knife.[6]

Marion remembers when her mother made the assignment; specifying Renderbrook's disposition on paper was almost like seeing it go for Jean Chappell. "It hurt her and she was sad about it," Marion said. "She said, 'Well, it's not mine anymore,' and it almost made me cry because she felt so very deeply about not having that ranch anymore."

Longtime office manager T. B. Zellner died April 1, 1966, and then for a few years the grim reaper appeared satisfied.

As the old faces departed, new ones appeared. Frank Cave took over some of W. F. Eisenberg's responsibilities so Eisenberg could slow down,[7] and as the decade of the sixties rolled past the halfway mark, Frank Chappell began casting about for a general manager to handle the sprawling Spade operations. Chappell recognized that ranching was no longer the same industry it had been in W. L.'s day, nor even in his own formative years. If the Spades were to survive and prosper in the future, they would need modern, innovative management. Chappell sought the best help he could get.

"It took all the courage and money I had," he would later quip, but he found his man in W. J. "Dub" Waldrip. Waldrip was certainly not the typical old-time ranch manager; he held a Ph.D. from Texas A&M University and was still affiliated with A&M through a position on the Texas Agricultural Experiment Station staff.[8] Chappell heard of Waldrip through cowman friends, much as his grandfather and great-grandfather had been put on to Uncle Dick Arnett. And more like Arnett than a typical Ph.D., Waldrip wasn't sequestered away in a classroom or academic office. Chappell found him in charge of the Texas Experimental Ranch that he had helped establish on Swenson Cattle Company land near Throckmorton. He first approached Waldrip with a proposal in early February of 1967. "I asked him what it would cost to hire him away from there," Chappell said. "When he told me, I swallowed hard and agreed to it."

An easy repartee quickly grew up between the two men. For his part, Waldrip took to calling Frank Chappell "Professor," sort of a touché to one of Chappell's own jokes.[9] As Waldrip explained it, Chappell called him one day. "Is this Doctor Waldrip?" Chappell asked, poking fun at the title Waldrip earned but never uses.

"Yes, it is," Waldrip answered.

"Well, this is Professor Chappell." Ever since, Chappell was "the perfessor."

Actually, Waldrip didn't accept the Spades' offer immediately. His natural inclination is to study an idea carefully before accepting or rejecting it, and he didn't stray from that path in what would prove to be one of the major decisions of his life.

"I gave the offer lots of serious consideration," Waldrip recalls, up to and including visiting both Renderbrook and the Chappell Spade at Tucumcari.[10] Frank Chappell had previously bought his sister's share of the old Bell Ranch acreage, but it would continue to be operated in conjunction with Renderbrook, so Waldrip was careful to find out what he might be getting into there as well as in Texas. He liked what he saw both places.

"From the beginning," Waldrip reminisces, "I could see that there were good people associated with the Spades," from the owners through the management and right on down to the cowhands. He signed on effective May 1, 1967, and almost immediately began making changes, a perilous practice on an outfit as long established and steeped in tradition as Renderbrook. In fact, one of Waldrip's first plans was to fly in the face of a half-century of that tradition by switching to crossbred cattle instead of the venerable straight Herefords so long associated with ranching in West Texas. It could have had a disastrous effect, but it didn't, because Waldrip had his people pretty well figured out. Aside from the semi-retired Otto Jones, the key was Shorty Northcutt, who had graduated to resident manager at Renderbrook just months before. As next in command, he was the one who would have to carry out the changes Waldrip was planning.

"Happily," Waldrip says, "a lot of our ideas were similar. . . . I already had a pretty good idea of some of the changes that needed to be made, and with Shorty's help, we started making some fairly soon after I got there."

The biggest change, to Waldrip's way of thinking, was Renderbrook's crossbreeding program. "We didn't do that overnight," he explains, "but we did a lot of looking and testing and trying out."

The first bovine crossbred to run on Renderbrook since the breed-up from Durham to Hereford half a century earlier was the ubiquitous black baldy. This Hereford-Angus cross, with color lines similar to the Hereford but in black and white rather than red and white, served to introduce many a cowman to crossbreeding. The performance advantage of crosses over straight-breds had been known to the academic community long years before it was commonly accepted by producers. The key was heterosis, or "hybrid vigor," in which the product of two dissimilar parents proves superior to either. Cattle breeds by the very nature of exclusivity and registration became closed clubs in the genetic sense, so simply crossing individuals from two different breeds was enough to produce measurable heterosis in the early days of crossbreeding.

That was fortunate for the future of the practice, at least in West Texas, because few tradition-bound stockmen were willing to reach far from their roots to test it. For many Hereford breeders even the coal-black Angus bordered on being an abomination though it was developed in the same northern British Isles as their own breed. The humpy, loose-hided "Braymer" was totally out of the question in terms of testing the crossbreeding water; they'd sooner breed their precious red cows to a camel. But the black baldface wasn't so much a test of the concept on Renderbrook as a study of the right sort of crossbreeding combination. Northcutt was running black baldies on his own ranch, and by the time they first hit the ground at Renderbrook, Waldrip and team were already light-years ahead in the practice. They weren't looking for a simple two-way cross or content to stop even with a three-way animal.

"I knew all along we would need four," Waldrip explains. "To get the full shot of hybrid vigor with each cross, you just have to have at least four breeds of cattle in the mix."

They had the Hereford to begin with, and the Angus component was natural, but in 1967 there weren't many beef breeds available in the U.S. from which to choose a third cross. Waldrip turned to the research community for help, traveling to Iowa State University and the government research station at Clay Center, Nebraska, to consult with cattle and carcass experts.

"It didn't take long to figure out that to stay in business, we were going to have to improve our weaning weights, probably change the kind of carcass we were producing, and change the way we marketed our cattle."

Based on the advice of the experts "and with a lot of study and research and taking advantage of other people's mistakes," Waldrip settled on the Brown Swiss to bring Renderbrook's crossbreeding program up to three breeds. At that point he took another step that the traditional ranching business had not yet begun to employ with any regularity. "Even in 1968 or 1969 with the first calves," Waldrip remembered, "as soon as we got them weaned we started to test them."

The first Spade calves to be performance tested came off the Chappell Spade in New Mexico and went to a feedlot carcass evaluation test at Hatch, New Mexico, and later Chaves County Feedyards at Roswell. There they were fed in commercial fashion with the addition of careful record-keeping on both their live performance and the carcasses they produced.

"We found approximately what we expected," Waldrip said, "except that it exceeded even our fondest expectations in some respects." And the results were self-confirming. "There was a straight-line regression," he explained, "with the black baldfaces fitting halfway in between the straight-bred animal and the Swiss cross in every test we ran."

That still left the question of what breed to use for the fourth cross, but the answer was coming closer by the day as the domestic cattle business suddenly exploded in diversity with an invasion of European "exotic" breeds. The big, white Charolais from France had ranked as the only such exotic of consequence within U.S. borders for many years, but as the sixties drew to a close other Continental breeds began to wash up on the nation's shores. Among those that would take firm root were the Chianina from Italy, the Limousin from France and the Simmental from Switzerland.

"We looked at all of them," Waldrip recalls. "We even made trips to Europe to see what they were doing over there."

Canada, with a somewhat more European focus than the U.S., was quicker to accept the Continental animals, both from a standpoint of attitudes and legal access. Once they were in Canada, it was a much more manageable step to bring them across the border than to import them directly from Europe. So Waldrip went to Canada. "We looked at the animals and at performance records where we could find them. Finally we decided, on the basis not only of growth but also the mothering ability of the cow, that we'd go with the Simmental. We've never been sorry for that decision."

That gave the Spade operation a terminal cross made up of Hereford, Swiss, Angus and Simmental, with no breed exceeding 9/16 of the total in any animal. It was apparently the first four-way cross consisting of two British and two Swiss cattle breeds.

But it wasn't totally smooth sailing, at least at first. Renderbrook had kept a small registered Hereford herd since 1937 when Otto Jones elected to breed his own replacement bulls rather than buy them from outside as had been the practice up to that point. It never became an end in itself, and Jones' refusal to follow the forties and fifties fad for little "watchfob" Herefords probably kept Spade cattle from figuring in the registered Hereford business to any major degree. That stubborn insistence on big, rugged cattle—

mostly the old Anxiety 4th strain—also spared Renderbrook and the Spades any of the dwarfism problems that
threatened to wreck the breed when the fascination for tiny
bulls finally produced its inevitable side effect. So Renderbrook had a strong and proven source for good quality
Hereford cows. Angus were also readily available as were
Brown Swiss, though to a lesser degree. Simmental cattle,
however, were still few and far between when Dub Waldrip
settled on them as the fourth breed in his crossing program.

The Spades were forced to raise their own. They started
in 1969 by artificially inseminating some of Renderbrook's
best Hereford cows, using semen from the top bulls in the
Simmental breed.

"By 1970 we were blowin' and goin'," Waldrip says, and
shortly afterward the Spades imported their first and only
purebred stock from overseas. There were five bulls and
thirteen heifers in all. "We couldn't get them from the Continent, but there were cattle from the Continent in Great
Britain and we could import their offspring." The breed-up
from Hereford cross cattle continued and as the offspring
from these approached Simmental status some of the best
of them joined the purebred imports in an embryo transplant program. That state-of-the-art endeavor involved artificially inseminating top donor cows and then flushing
their fertilized embryos for transplantation into other,
lesser cows. Instead of producing one calf a year and carrying it to term, a transplant donor can produce one or
more embryos per estrus cycle; these embryos are then carried by recipient or host cows, freeing the donor to provide
more desirable embryos at the next heat cycle.

Even for the best transplant technicians, the percentage
of live births to embryos has never been nearly as high as
natural breeding, but there are so many more potential embryos that the process provides rapid expansion of other-

Dub Waldrip (left) and Otto Jones in the late 1960s. Below, the
Renderbrook chain of command shares lunch at the roundup
chuckwagon. Left to right: Frank Chappell, Dub Waldrip and
Shortry Northcutt (Spade Ranches Collection).

wise limited bloodlines. That, of course, was Waldrip's goal, and the growing Spade Simmental herd was so successful in reaching it that there were enough surplus females by 1973 to conduct the first of a short series of production sales.

"We sold 100 females," Waldrip remembers, "and they averaged something over $3000 apiece, which we thought was really outstanding for that time."

The 1974 sale did even better. Also featuring a hundred head, it averaged more than $5000, over a half-million dollars. Waldrip credited the American Simmental Association and its policies for much of that success. The association, he explained, "was formed more by practical, performance-oriented commercial cow people, so their rules and regulations were based more on economic traits than most other breed programs." ASA rules go so far as to require performance testing as a condition of registration. "I think that helped the breed, and it helped us to identify the better cattle in the breed," Waldrip says.

But even that wasn't enough to save the Spades' 1975 production sale. It's unlikely anything could have. The cattle market had peaked in the summer of 1973 with light feeder steers bringing well over $75 per hundredweight and fed steers nearly $60 coming out of Texas Panhandle feedlots. The next week both fats and feeders fell as far as it had taken them two weeks to climb, and feeders dropped two more weeks' worth the week after that. It was an unbroken slide for another month, followed by a month of labored effort to recover ground it had taken only one week to lose. By early fall the market was in full retreat again and it tumbled for weeks until fed steers settled at $37 toward the first of June 1974. Average price on the spring crop of steer calves had sunk below the fat price for the first time in years, bottoming at about $36.

In a few weeks even those prices would look good as a brief rally collapsed and the cattle crash turned into a real bloodletting. Some producers who ordinarily sold their calf crops as feeders couldn't bear to take the loss at that stage and elected to retain ownership through the feedlot instead. Surely three or four months would be long enough for a market turnaround, they reasoned, and they could at least break even. As it turned out, they just lost twice as much money.

Such disaster on the commercial cattle market inevitably infected the purebred trade as well; it was just delayed a bit. Well before the 1975 Spade sale, however, the season's rounds of registered bull sales were showing the symptoms. One after another fell short of their 1974 marks. Just as the 1973 and 1974 Spade sales had exceeded expectations in high prices, the 1975 version fell even flatter than expected. The 1975 sale, Waldrip remembered, "was probably twenty percent of what the 1974 sale had been."[12]

It was to be the operation's last real Simmental production sale, though there was a "partial dispersal" about three years later as numbers were trimmed to the level needed to produce bulls for the commercial crossbreeding program. The Spades were never really active in the purebred business again. It had served its purpose for them, providing a way to recoup the costs of developing a Simmental herd at a time when the Swiss exotics were scarce, but Renderbrook and its sister operations had always been commercial outfits first and foremost. From 1975 on, the purebred Simmental herd would join the purebred Hereford herd in relative obscurity.

While all this was underway, Waldrip was also modernizing Renderbrook's grazing management program. From the beginning, he and Shorty Northcutt agreed that the previous practice of continuous grazing in large pastures no longer served the ranch's needs. It took "a year or two" to plan and install the new rotational grazing scheme, in part because it required fencing to provide more and smaller pastures. In the end it resembled a "Merrill-type deferred rotation system," in Waldrip's words, but with a twist. The Merrill plan, devised by former Sonora Experiment Station resident director Dr. Leo Merrill, involves three herds rotated through four pastures. One pasture is always rested or freed from grazing pressure while the livestock graze the other three. One by one, each pasture gets its turn at rest.

Waldrip's twist was "a series of systems in which we superimposed the breeding rotation on top of the grazing rotation. "It's not complicated," Waldrip has said, "but it's difficult to explain."

In 1971, after helping to put the grazing program into place and get the Simmental breed-up underway, Shorty Northcutt retired from his position as resident ranch manager.

"Thank goodness he'd done a good job of raising an awfully good cowman," Waldrip remarked, "because we put Bob Northcutt, Shorty's son, into the position. In my opinion, Bob's probably the best ranch manager in the business."

Bob Northcutt's ability to step into his father's boots without breaking stride undoubtedly helped the entire operation through a trying period. In addition to the elder Northcutt's retirement, the Spade family also lost three other members, the latter permanently. Dee Bassham passed away on April 26, 1971, and Elise Keeney on August 20.[13] The Keeney branch of the family no longer had direct ties to Renderbrook, but they were still very much family. Also very much family, though not blood kin, was W. F. Eisenberg. Despite gradually slowing down in the late sixties, Eisenberg never actually retired. When he passed away on the sixth of January, 1972, he was still actively engaged in Spade management.[14]

His death left a void in the Lubbock office that grew even larger when Frank Chappell decided to move back to Connecticut. To fill it, Waldrip left Renderbrook and Colorado City after four years, taking up residence in Lubbock and taking over the Lubbock office.

A Century Under The Spade Brand

12

DESPITE the violent price crash of 1973 and 1974, Waldrip assessed the cattle business as "really pretty good" overall during the seventies.[1] At least it worked out that way for Renderbrook and the Spades. With their advanced crossbreeding program, they were well positioned to take advantage of the price boom that was underway at decade's end.

Feeder cattle prices in 1979 soared to over $100 per hundredweight and fed steers nudged $80 before the two classes closed the year at about $90 and $70, respectively. It was a bit like being lulled to sleep by a thief so he can rob you blind.[2]

"The eighties saw the return of some pretty tough times in the business," Waldrip recalls.[3] Fed cattle prices through both 1980 and '81 remained generally at or above the mid-sixties. The Spades had adopted a policy of carrying their cattle through the feedlot because of Waldrip's conviction that multiple crosses such as they were producing weren't earning the price consideration they deserved from feeder buyers. It can be a rewarding marketing method under the right circumstances, and it was right in the early 1980s as feeder cattle prices slipped from their heady late-seventies highs. The best 400- to 500-pound steers slipped from about $94 at the beginning of 1980 to the mid-sixties by the end of 1981. They never broke $70 in 1982 and barely pulled back up to $72 by the end of 1983.

By then, however, poor weather and Washington politics had combined to drag the feedlot end of the business down, too. The winter of 1982–1983 had been a snowy, icy affair, causing cattle feeders performance loss and considerable death. Then dry weather in the Cornbelt the following summer boosted grain prices, increasing the feeders' costs. To add to the damage, the federal government chose that time to implement its "payment-in-kind" or "PIK" program. A dual effort to reduce the growing stockpiles of surplus commodities (bought and stored at taxpayer expense) and to cut down on cash farm subsidies (which went, after all, to buy more surplus), the PIK program paid farmers in commodities in lieu of legal tender. It worked to the extent that grain prices edged up even more.

Then came the bitterly cold winter of 1983–1984. In the space of a few hours in mid-December the weather changed from balmy shirtsleeve temperatures to bitter cold as the first in a series of Arctic fronts blew across the Texas Panhandle, down through the Colorado and Concho country, and finally blanketed the state. The bitter cold would last until after the first of the year and shatter low temperature records throughout the region. Dirt stock tanks not only froze over—a rare enough event—but the ice pack became thick enough to support cattle and horses as the thirsty animals ventured out onto the slick surface in search of a drink. Watering holes several feet wide and twice as long laboriously chopped in the ice froze up almost before they were finished. Death losses were relatively light, mostly because the vicious storms were as dry as they were cold. Had the spell been as wet as the previous year's, though, dead livestock would have littered ranches, stockfarms and feedlots throughout the northern two-thirds of the state. The dryness was a continuation of a trend that had begun earlier in 1983, though in a broader sense it may actually have started well before that. In the spring of 1982 Waldrip committed to tape something of a "state of the Spade" report, assessing conditions as they existed at the time. He reflected then on "a disastrous period" of weather "last year and the year before." He said, in fact, "at Renderbrook we've had about three years of below-average conditions and last year we lost some grass to the extreme heat and dry weather." He predicted that it would take "a long period of careful management" to recover the lost forage.[4]

The ranch had enjoyed, however, a "very favorable climate" during the intervening fall of '82, which may be a major reason why the 1980s drouth is generally measured from 1983 instead of 1980 or even earlier. Another reason could be that the severity and apparent suddenness of the drouth's onset in 1983 attracted such undivided attention that the earlier feelers seemed mild by comparison. Waldrip considered the eighties dry spell "a duplication of the drouth of the fifties." The main difference, he felt, was that it wasn't nearly as widespread geographically, "but it was certainly bad where it occurred, and we seemed to be right in the middle of it."[5]

Renderbrook, Waldrip recalls, "started moving cattle in the mid-summer of 1983 and before we started coming back home with them we were down to something like 143 cows.

We still had some of our heifers and some of our sheep, and on 200 sections even that was probably more than we should have been carrying."

A costly and complicating factor for the Spades was that they dared not lose the seed stock for their complex breeding program. "We made a special effort to hang onto most of our cows. We had them scattered over a pretty wide area from '83 to '85." Some were on the blackland near Granbury, others on the Chappell Spade in New Mexico and on an adjoining lease they called the Clabber Hill Spade. That particular outfit was another part of the old Bell Ranch, bought by Sam Arnett and still in his family. And that wasn't all. "We had quite a few cattle up in the Clarendon area and we ended up with quite a few more on the Wagon Creek Spade near Throckmorton after we got it leased." Still more Renderbrook cows grazed Keeney family country near Sundown and Whiteface on the Plains.

"It wasn't what you would call an economical operation, especially with the shape the cattle business was in . . . but we did manage to hang onto a lot of our cows, and in 1985 and '86, especially in '86, we got home with quite a few, most of them young cattle." One facet of the drouth that nagged at Waldrip personally was that Renderbrook went into that period while he was serving as president of the National Cattlemen's Association. He worried over accepting the post at least a full year before it was officially offered.

"As most of you know," he said in what was to be a newsletter to Spade "participants" in 1982, "I was elected in February to the position of first vice president of the NCA, which I presume is the first step in becoming president. . . . This is quite an honor and I appreciate it, but I'm not sure that it was the proper thing to do." Waldrip said he probably wouldn't have accepted the job "had it not been for the enthusiastic support from the major partners, particularly at Professor Chappell's urging. So if things go to pot while I'm looking after the national association, you can all blame Professor Chappell.[6]

"Seriously," he continued, "if it weren't for the outstanding help at each of the ranches, there would be no way that I could even consider such a task. We're extremely fortunate to have possibly the best on-site management of any ranch in the country."

With those misgivings beforehand, it isn't surprising that Waldrip chided himself a few years later for "maybe not looking after things as closely as I should have" in 1983.[7] But he was apparently alone in that assessment. Chappell in particular could find nothing to regret about Waldrip's service as NCA president despite the unfortunate timing. On the contrary, Chappell took pride in the association's selection of the Spade manager to fill its highest elected post.[8] Though he might never have said it in so many words, he recognized that at the very least it represented an industry-wide vote of confidence in his own selection of Waldrip years before.

The final years of Renderbrook's first century were an abrupt reversal of the early eighties in terms of weather and market. As it had in the fifties and before, the dry weather surrendered to a wetter than normal period—two full years, in fact, of exceptional, well-timed rainfall. The change began farther west, where the drouth had begun. The first sign came in late spring 1984, when the Davis Mountains enjoyed a deluge that broke the long dry spell but literally washed away roads and bridges in the process. Before long the clouds crept out of the mountains onto the flat expanse of the Trans-Pecos and began moving eastward. It would be the better part of a year before Renderbrook felt the effects, but when the rains finally did come it was like turning on a tap. Bountiful precipitation fell with rare regularity through 1985 and 1986, then lapped over into 1987. Rangeland that had lain bare as pavement sprouted weeds, then grass, including high-succession species in profusion unmatched for decades.

The rains slackened later and by 1988 tanks dependent upon runoff began to go dangerously low again, but some of the blame could be laid to abundance as well as scarcity— so much turf had grown while it rained that it took a genuine downpour to run water, and those just weren't to be had.

Renderbrook's centennial year began under skies that hadn't produced a good rain in months. The big question was whether it was the beginning of a new drouth, a resumption of the old one, or just a return to normal West Texas weather.

The answer would have a profound effect on livestock markets. Both sheep and cattle prices had seen a renaissance from about the mid-eighties on. Sheep led the advance, particularly fine-wool sheep like those on Renderbrook. A number of factors combined to boost lamb and wool prices, but the bottom line was that demand outran supply. The lion's share of the nation's fine-wool sheep production can be found in West Central Texas, and a huge chunk of that output had been curtailed by the drouth. The sheep were gone and there was literally nowhere to turn for replacements in any numbers. They would have to grow back.

Toward the middle of the decade, international trade developments boosted demand for fine wool and put an even tighter squeeze on supplies when both mainland China and the Soviet Union entered the world market as buyers. A stockpile of Australian fine wool had kept a practical lid on the worldwide price of the commodity for years, but that surplus was absorbed almost overnight when the eastern giants became players.

By the beginning of the 1987 spring wool season the effect of the increased demand had begun to show clearly in the prices buyers paid for raw "greasy" wool; better offerings that had been considered standouts at just over a dollar a pound a couple of years before were suddenly bringing $2. The opening of the 1988 spring season saw unheard-of $3 bids, and the best Renderbrook clip sold for $3.30.[9]

Cattle have remained Renderbrook's primary product, however, and the latter half of the eighties were kind to that market as well, but the early '80s were problem years. Supply and demand are the keys. One generally acknowledged reason for the soft cattle markets early in the decade was reduced demand brought on in part by health conscious consumers who were concerned about reported hazards of eating too much beef. In the late '70s, U.S. government panels warned Americans about the alleged dangers of red meat, and lobbying groups across the country added to the furor. Heart disease, cancer, even aggressive behavior were blamed on meat. The campaign was effective. Red meat consumption began to tail off and prices fell. Eventually cattlemen began to feel the pinch, prompting one of the deepest and most protracted herd liquidation cycles on record. By January 1, 1986, the nation's beef cow numbers had fallen shy of the lowest point previously seen in the official inventory's quarter-century history. Rebuilding had not begin in earnest two years later.

In the anti-meat campaign's apparent success, however, also lay the seeds of its eventual failure. First poultry, then pork, and finally the sprawling, disjointed and fiercely independent cattle industry began fighting back. Market research led to leaner products and medical research led to

evidence that many of the claims about the hazards of eating meat were either overblown, misstated or false.

Feeder cattle once again climbed to levels well above a
dollar a pound or $100 per hundredweight, and in the
spring of 1988 the cost of good young replacement cows
soared to more than $1000 per head in some special sales.
Dry conditions later rolled those prices back to less heady
levels but did little to trim the value of stocker and feeder
calves. Fed cattle coming out of West Texas lots also shared
in the prosperity; the early weeks of 1989 saw fed steers
bringing close to $80 per hundredweight.

It was a fitting way to close out Renderbrook's first century, stout prices providing something to celebrate and dry
weather as a counterpoint to keep the celebration in per-
spective. The juxtaposition of the two serves as a reminder
that ranching is always just an inch of rain away from prosperity or a few cents a pound away from financial disaster.
Renderbrook had seen both extremes more than once in its
hundred years under the Spade brand.

The ranch that barbed wire built was barely fenced when
I. L. Ellwood and his oldest son first scouted it in the summer of 1889. Its watering places were mostly those that
nature provided, and roundups had much in common with
the cow-hunts that preceded the short period of open range
empire then drawing to a close. Remnants of buffalo hides
still remained near the old Taylor Barr dugout at Renderbrook Spring, and the flag may still have flown over historic
old Fort Concho, depending upon the precise date of the
Ellwoods' visit. It wasn't until June 20, 1889, with the band
playing "The Girl I Left Behind Me," that Fort Concho's
complement of troops marched away for the last time. One
soldier who wasn't with them was Captain Joseph Rendlebrock. He had died in March of that very year after a decade
of retirement.[10]

Over the next ten decades Renderbrook would evolve into as modern a ranch as any in the Southwest, and far more modern than many. Planned grazing, systematic brush control and scientifically selected breeding rotations were put in place at Renderbrook when the concepts were still heresy to many ranchers, and the outfit instituted some of the earliest embryo transplanting in the industry.

Technology and time changed the face of ranching at Renderbrook. At its heart, however, the ranch has always been land and people. Colonel Isaac Ellwood, whose $265 investment in a neighbor's good idea made him a millionaire many times over, lived his life in such a way that thousands of people turned out to mourn his passing. W. L. Ellwood contributed his own irrepressible spirit to the enterprise, and he left as fond an impression as had his father in the memories of those who knew him.[11] Just as critical to the history of Renderbrook were the Arnetts, Otto Jones and his family, the Northcutts, Swanns, McClellans, Eisenbergs, Boatwrights, Russells, Arnolds, Sorrells, Hocks, and many others past and present. All gave something of themselves to the outfit, to the brand and to the land.

It is the land, however, that has made Renderbrook. The land gives the ranch its character, provides its products and imposes its limitations. Renderbrook has endured the drouths and bloomed in the bountiful times. It will continue to in the next century.

Notes

1—Cool Water and Cold Steel

1. Captain Joseph Rendlebrock, scouting report filed at Fort Concho, Texas, 21 February 1872, transcript in Fort Concho archives, San Angelo, Texas. All subsequent quotations from Rendlebrock are from this report.

2. Francis B. Heitman, *Historical Register and Dictionary of the United States Army* (Washington, D.C.: U.S. Government Printing Office, 1903), p. 823.

3. A photograph of Renderbrook spring house, circa 1900, clearly shows walnut trees of advanced age only about three decades after Rendlebrock's discovery. Photo provided by Marion Bassham, Colorado City, Texas.

4. R. C. Hopping, "Colonel Isaac L. Ellwood and William L. Ellwood," original manuscript in the Southwest Collection, Texas Tech University, Lubbock, Texas, pp. 1–2 (hereafter cited as Hopping, "The Ellwoods"). An edited version of this manuscript appears in *The Museum Journal* (Lubbock: The West Texas Museum Assn., Texas Technological College, 1962), volume 4. Hopping served as a land agent for the Ellwood interests during the colonization of their Texas Panhandle land in the 1920s and '30s, and became closely associated with the family and its history.

5. Henry D. and Frances T. McCallum, *The Wire That Fenced the West* (Norman: University of Oklahoma Press, 1965), pp. 3–28.

6. *Ibid.*, pp. 28–31.

7. Mary Isabel Brush, "John W. Gates Tells How Col. Ellwood and His Wife Made World's First Barbed Wire With a Coffee Mill," *Chicago Sunday Tribune*, 18 September 1910; H. D. and F. T. McCallum, *The Wire*, p. 32.

8. *Ibid.*, p. 38.

9. *Ibid.*, p. 32.

10. *Ibid.*, p. 32.

11. *Ibid.*, p. 32.

12. *Ibid.*, p. 36.

13. *Ibid.*, p. 38.

14. *Ibid.*, pp. 39–40.
15. *Ibid.*, pp. 44–45.

2—The Opening of West Texas

1. T. R. Fehrenbach, *Lone Star: A History of Texas and the Texans* (New York: American Legacy Press, 1968), pp. 538–540; J. Evetts Haley, *Fort Concho and the Texas Frontier* (San Angelo: San Angelo Standard-Times, 1952), pp. 176–178; Mildred P. Mayhall, *Indian Wars of Texas* (Waco: Texian Press, 1965), pp. 69–76. The account of the Warren Wagon Train Raid (or Salt Creek Massacre) and subsequent events are synthesized from these sources.

2. Fehrenbach, *Lone Star*, pp. 547–550; Haley, *Fort Concho*, pp. 204–226; Mayhall, *Indian Wars*, pp. 172–183. The accounts of MacKenzie's 1872 scouts and the 1874 campaign, including the Palo Duro raid, are taken from these sources. Fehrenbach and Mayhall date the Palo Duro raid on September 28. Haley gives the date as September 27.

3. Haley, *Fort Concho*, pp. 116–117.

4. Paul H. Carlson, *Texas Woollybacks* (College Station: Texas A&M University Press, 1982), p. 102.

5. Hopping, "The Ellwoods," p. 36.

6. Joe Pickle, *Gettin' Started* (Big Spring, Texas: Howard County Heritage Museum, 1980), p. 283.

7. *Ibid.*, p. 109.

8. R. H. Looney, "History of Colorado, Texas," *Lore and Legend* (Colorado City, Texas: Colorado City Record, 1976), pp. 7–23.

9. Hopping, "The Ellwoods," p. 36.

10. J. Marvin Hunter, *The Trail Drivers of Texas* (Austin: University of Texas Press, 1985), pp. 721–729, 1029-1031. The account of D. H. and J. W. Snyder, except where otherwise noted, is drawn from these two articles in Hunter's compilation, the latter a brief autobiographical tract by D. H. Snyder himself.

11. Redemption certificate number 306, issued by Texas State Comptroller W. M. Brown, Austin, Texas, 3 May 1882, in Southwest Collection, Texas Tech University, Lubbock, Texas; warranty deeds transferring various tracts of land from D. H. and J. W. Snyder to I. L. Ellwood, 18 and 19 February 1890, at Southwest Collection, Lubbock.

12. Hopping, "The Ellwoods," pp. 35–36.

3—Birth of an Empire

1. Hopping, "The Ellwoods," p. 33.
2. *Ibid.*, p. 34.
3. *Ibid.*, p. 36.
4. *Ibid.*
5. *Ibid.*, p. 37.
6. R. H. Looney, "History of Colorado, Texas."
7. J. Evetts Haley, *The XIT Ranch of Texas* (Norman: University of Oklahoma Press, 1953), p. 55.
8. *Ibid.*
9. *Ibid.*
10. Hopping, "The Ellwoods," pp. 39–42.
11. *Ibid.*, pp. 44–45.
12. Details of D. N. Arnett's life are drawn from an anonymous tract titled "Sketch of D.N. Arnett's Life," obtained from W. J. "Dub" Waldrip, Spade Ranches general manager (copy in author's possession).
13. Fehrenbach, *Lone Star*, pp. 424–426.
14. Hopping, "The Ellwoods," pp. 46–50.
15. *Ibid.*, p. 49.
16. *Ibid.*, pp. 49–50.

4—Colonel Ike

1. Hopping, "The Ellwoods," p. 16.
2. H. D. and F. T. McCallum, *The Wire*, pp. 103, 222.
3. *Ibid.*, pp. 65–67.
4. *Ibid.*, pp. 68–72.
5. *Ibid.*, p. 74.
6. *Ibid.*, p. 78.
7. *Ibid.*, p. 83.
8. *Ibid.*, pp. 106–107.
9. *Ibid.*, pp. 102–103.
10. Mary Isabel Brush, "John W. Gates. . . ."
11. H. D. and F. T. McCallum, *The Wire*, pp. 100–101.
12. Frank Chappell, interview with author, San Angelo, Texas, July 1988.
13. H. D. and F. T. McCallum, *The Wire*, p. 99; Brush, "John W. Gates . . ."; Hopping, "The Ellwoods," p. 16.

14. Frank Chappell, interview with author, San Angelo, Texas, July 1988.

15. Handwritten letter to I. L. Ellwood, correspondent's signature illegible (N. Weber?), Kansas, 27 November 1896.

16. Vernon Russell, letter to I. L. Ellwood, Great Bend, Kansas, 28 May 1897.

17. Hopping, "The Ellwoods," pp. 17, 58.

18. *Ibid.*, p. 55.

19. Otto F. Jones, interview taped by Elmer Kelton, 29 July 1971, Colorado City, Texas, copy in Southwest Collection, Texas Tech University, Lubbock, Texas.

20. *Ibid.*

21. H. D. and F. T. McCallum, *The Wire*, p. 102.

22. Hopping, "The Ellwoods," p. 59.

5—Expansion

1. Hopping, "The Ellwoods," pp. 60–61.

2. The following account of the Ellwoods' expansion in the Texas Panhandle is drawn from Hopping's "The Ellwoods," pp. 53–55, 84–86, 88, 90–91.

3. *Ibid.*, pp. 71–72.

4. Frank Chappell, interview with author, Renderbrook Ranch, Summer 1986.

5. Hopping, "The Ellwoods," p. 68.

6. *Ibid.*, p. 69.

7. *Ibid.*, pp. 68, 74.

8. *Ibid.*, p. 103.

9. *Ibid.*, p. 70.

10. *Ibid.*, pp. 52–57.

11. *Ibid.*, p. 94; see also Brush, "John W. Gates. . . ."

12. Hopping, "The Ellwoods," p. 94.

13. *Ibid.*, p. 101; Brush, "John W. Gates. . . ."

14. Hopping, "The Ellwoods," p. 101.

15. *Ibid.*, p. 73.

6—Cowmen, Cattle and Horseflesh

1. Otto Jones, interview taped by E. Kelton.

2. Hopping, "The Ellwoods," pp. 74–75; Marion Chappell

Bassham, interview taped by author, 5 April 1986, Colorado City, Texas, original in author's possession.

3. Hopping, "The Ellwoods," pp. 75–79.
4. Otto Jones, interview taped by E. Kelton.
5. *Ibid.*
6. *Ibid.*
7. Frank Chappell, interview with author, Renderbrook Ranch, summer 1986. This four-word notation can be quoted by any number of individuals familiar with Jones or the Spade Ranches, but the whereabouts of the "day book" in which it was written is unknown. All of Jones' pocket notebooks are thought to have been preserved in a group, but the collection has not been located. Jones transcribed and fleshed out some of his daily notations in longhand on yellow legal pads, and excerpts on scraps of paper, envelopes, etc. These reminiscent entries are not dated. (Hereafter cited as Jones, "Recollections.") Undated copies were provided by Jones' daughter, Pauline Jones Cauble, and are in the possession of the author.
8. Otto Jones, interview taped by Virgil Lawyer, 30 December 1959, Colorado City, Texas, copy in Southwest Collection, Texas Tech University, Lubbock, Texas.
9. Jones, interview taped by E. Kelton.
10. Jones, interview taped by V. Lawyer.
11. Otto Jones, letter to grandson Ray Franklin Kayser, 20 February 1975, copy in author's possession.
12. Jones, "Recollections."
13. *Ibid.*
14. *Ibid.*
15. Jones, interview taped by E. Kelton.
16. Jones, interview taped by V. Lawyer.
17. Jones, "Recollections."
18. Jones, interview taped by V. Lawyer.
19. *Ibid.*
20. *Ibid.*
21. *Ibid.*
22. *Ibid.*
23. Bassham, interview taped by author.
24. Jones, interview taped by V. Lawyer.
25. *Ibid.*
26. *Ibid.*

27. Jones, interview taped by E. Kelton.
28. *Ibid.*
29. Charles G. Scruggs, *The Peaceful Atom and the Deadly Fly* (Austin, Texas: The Pemberton Press, 1975); W. J. "Dub" Waldrip, interview with author, fall 1988, Lubbock, Texas.
30. Jones "Recollections."
31. Jones, interview taped by E. Kelton.
32. *Ibid.*
33. *Ibid.*

7—Colonization and the Turning of a Page

1. Jones, interview taped by E. Kelton.
2. *Ibid.*
3. *Ibid.*
4. Jones, interview taped by V. Lawyer.
5. Jones "Recollections."
6. *Ibid.*
7. *Ibid.*
8. *Ibid.*
9. Jones, interview taped by V. Lawyer.
10. Hopping, "The Ellwoods," p. 63.
11. Ralph Stein, *The American Automobile* (New York: Random House), p. 146.
12. Hopping, "The Ellwoods," pp. 63–65.
13. *Ibid.*, p. 103.
14. *Ibid.*, pp. 103–105.
15. *Ibid.*, p. 73.
16. *Ibid.*, p. 110.
17. *Ibid.* pp. 115–117.
18. *Ibid.*, pp. 117–118.
19. *Ibid.*, 120-121. The account of the colonization of the Spade Ranches is taken from Hopping, "The Ellwoods," pp. 120–138.
20. *Ibid.*, pp. 139–140.

8—Dust Bowl Days

1. Hopping, "The Ellwoods," pp. 140–143.
2. Frank Chappell, interview with author, Renderbrook Ranch, summer 1986.

3. Jones, interview taped by V. Lawyer.

4. *Ibid.*

5. Interview with Renderbrook cowboys of the 1930s to 1950s, taped by author, 14 November 1986, Renderbrook Ranch.

6. Jones, interview taped by V. Lawyer.

7. Interview with cowboys, taped by author.

8. Jones, interview taped by V. Lawyer; Jones, interview taped by E. Kelton; Jones, "Recollections."

9. Jones, interview taped by V. Lawyer.

10. Jones, interview taped by E. Kelton.

11. Jones, interview taped by V. Lawyer.

12. *Ibid.*

13. *Ibid.*

14. Frank Chappell, interview by author, Renderbrook Ranch, summer 1986.

9—High Times and Horse Wrecks

1. Interview with Renderbrook cowboys, taped by author. Unless otherwise noted, the following stories are drawn from this source.

2. Frank Chappell, interview by author, July 1986, San Angelo, Texas.

3. Bassham, interview taped by author. Unless otherwise noted, the following accounts involving Marion Bassham are drawn from this interview.

4. Interview with cowboys, taped by author.

5. Frank Chappell, interview by author, July, 1986, San Angelo, Texas. Unless otherwise noted, the following accounts involving Frank Chappell are drawn from this interview.

6. Waldrip, interview by author.

10—Clouds of War, None of Rain

1. J. E. "Shorty" Northcutt, interview by author, 19 December 1988, Colorado City, Texas.

2. Jones, interview taped by V. Lawyer.

3. *Ibid.*

4. Frank Chappell, interview by author, Renderbrook Ranch, summer 1986.

5. Jones, interview taped by V. Lawyer.
6. *Ibid.*
7. *Ibid.*
8. Jones, interview taped by E. Kelton; Waldrip, interview by author.
9. Ellwood Keeney, telephone interview by author, December 1988, Lubbock, Texas.
10. Roscoe Wilson, letter to Charles Gibbs, 22 May 1934; J. R. Pratt, letter to T. B. Zellner, 26 May 1934; Roscoe Wilson, letter to E. P. Ellwood, 28 May 1934; Roscoe Wilson, letter to E. P. Ellwood, 31 May 1934; Roscoe Wilson, letter to Charles Gibbs, 31 May 1934. All in Spade Ranches files, Lubbock, Texas.
11. W. F. Eisenberg, letter to Mrs. Frank H. (Jean Ellwood) Chappell, 31 July 1948, in Southwest Collection, Texas Tech University, Lubbock, Texas; also warranty deed accompanying same.
12. Hopping, "The Ellwoods," pp. 148–150.
13. Ellwood Keeney, telephone interview by author.
14. Northcutt, interview by author.
15. Jones, interview taped by V. Lawyer.
16. Elmer Kelton, "Spade Ranch Honors Three Of Its Longtime Employes," *San Angelo Standard Times*, 4 August 1957.

11—Fast-Paced Change

1. Northcutt, interview by author.
2. "Dry Cows on Spade Ranch Get 'One-Way Ticket' Out," *The Abilene Reporter-News*, 19 May 1968, p. 14–D.
3. Jones, interview taped by E. Kelton.
4. Jean Gillette, "Range Burning Test Eyed On Spade Tour," *San Angelo Standard-Times*, 10 May 1968, p. 11–A.
5. "Birth and Death Date List," Spade Ranches files, Lubbock, Texas.
6. Bassham, interview taped by author.
7. Waldrip, interview by author.
8. Frank Chappell, interview by author, summer 1988, San Angelo, Texas.
9. Waldrip, interview by author.
10. W. J. "Dub" Waldrip, recollections recorded and presented to author, summer 1988, in author's possession. The following

accounts quoting Waldrip, unless otherwise noted, are drawn from this source.

11. Cattle prices quoted in this account are compiled from various issues of *Livestock Weekly* (San Angelo), including graph of 1966-1977 prices printed in issue of 5 January 1978.

12. Waldrip, recorded recollections.

13. "Birth and Death Date List."

14. W. J. "Dub" Waldrip, interview by author, fall, 1986, Lubbock, Texas.

12—A Century Under The Spade Brand

1. Waldrip, recorded recollections.

2. Cattle prices quoted in this account are compiled from various issues of *Livestock Weekly*.

3. Waldrip, recorded recollections.

4. Waldrip, recorded dictation intended for newsletter, spring 1982, in author's possession.

5. Waldrip, recorded recollections.

6. Waldrip, recorded dictation.

7. Waldrip, recorded recollections.

8. Frank Chappell, interview by author, summer 1988.

9. Wool, lamb and cattle prices in this account are compiled from various issues of *Livestock Weekly*.

10. Heitman, *Historical Register and Dictionary of the United States Army*, p. 823.

11. Frank Chappell, interview by author, summer 1988.

Index

Brownwood, Texas, 39
Burnet County, Texas, 22
Bush & Tillar Ranch, 74

C Ranch, 68
Cameron, Texas, 35
Camp system, 61–63, 112,
139–140, 144
Canyon, Texas, 112–114
Capitol Syndicate, 33, 38
Carlsbad, New Mexico, 114
Carpenter, W.L., 34–35
Cattle: crossbreeding, 184–185,
194; dwarfism, 188;
performance testing of, 190;
price crash, 1970s, 190–191
Cavalry, Fourth, 1
Cave, Frank, 182
Chappell, Frank H., Jr., 153,
159–161, 167, 173, 182–183,
193, 198
Chappell, Frank H., Sr., 153
Chappell, Frank, III, 161
Chappell, Jenny, 161
Chappell, Marcia, 161
Chappell, Robert, 161
Chappell Coal and Lumber
Company, 153
Chappell Spade Ranch, 183, 186,
197
Chaves County feedyards, 186
Cheyenne, Wyoming, 22
Chianina cattle, 187
Christopher, Joe, 160
Chuckwagon, menu and cooks,
60, 80–84
Citizens National Bank of
Lubbock, 68, 127
Clabber Hill Ranch, 68
Clabber Hill Spade, 197
Clarendon, Texas, 197
Clay Center, Nebraska, 186
Clayton, Rube, 68

Cocinero, 82
Coke County, 23, 34, 37
Colorado City, Texas (Colorado,
Texas), 2, 20, 25, 29–31, 34,
39–40, 72, 75, 103, 105, 142,
153, 157, 159, 173, 193
Colorado Clipper, 19
Colorado River, 2, 7, 16, 18–20,
33, 92, 101, 157, 195
Columbia Patent Company, 46,
49, 52
Comanche Indians, 12, 15–18,
112
Concho River, 2, 3, 18–19, 22,
106, 195
Cornbelt, 195
Crossbreeding, cattle, 184–185,
194

Daly, James, 106
Davis Mountains, Texas, 198
DeKalb, Illinois, 5, 7–9, 11, 27,
33–34, 39–42, 48–49, 52, 55,
67–69, 74, 105–106, 112–113,
123–124
Denver, Colorado, 23
Donley County, Texas, 34, 56
Drouth: 24–25, 72, 199;
1916–1918, 72, 79, 102–103;
Dust Bowl, 129–133; 1950s,
167–170, 172–176; 1980s,
196–198
Durham cattle, 24, 34, 98
Dwarfism, in cattle, 188

Eisenberg, William F., "Will,"
124–129, 156, 161, 167,
170–171, 173–174, 182,
192–193, 202
El Paso, Texas, 114
Ellwood, E. Perry, 53, 68–69,
123–127, 134, 170–171,
173–174, 182, 192–193, 202